# The Job getting Formula

## For The Experienced Worker

A Simple 5-Step Secret To *Get A High-paying Job*...That Will Help *Pay Your Debt* And *Offer You The Good Life Full Of Fun*

## Sylvester Nkongho

# The Job getting Formula

## COPYRIGHT

ISBN: 10: 061557968X
ISBN-13: 978-0-615-57968-9

# The Job getting Formula

## PRAISES

"If you need a complete job-getting blueprint, then study this book."

---*Roland Kwemain, 2010 President, Junior Chamber International.*

"As someone who has spent over 25 years in corporate life and who has tasted both ends as a recruiter and as being recruited, you could say I am a poacher and gamekeeper of job hunting. This book by Sylvester draws on his personal experience which is always an inspiration. As every scientist knows, with a formula you get consistent output or results from quality and consistent inputs, all the time, without failure."

"Therefore, to get a high-paying job, you need to follow the formula in this book."

"We all know people who are experienced but stuck in situations that are not fulfilling. Either they have tried different programs of job search with no success, or all they want is a formula that gives them what they want. That is what Sylvester has succeeded in doing here – giving the formula and succinct, practical, easy-to-follow examples to ensure success. I hope you follow the formula and ensure success for yourself, your family and your community."

*--- Mike Awanayah, Founder Jesmax Ltd, United Kingdom.*

*(Formerly, Head of Talent & People Development, Diageo-Guinness Cameroon and Operations Manager at Guinness Nigeria, PLC)*

"I am so excited to say this... the Job-getting Formula just got me my dream job. It's an easy to read and step by step approach to make your résumé and cover letter stand out from the pool of applicants out there. I had to redo my résumé and my cover letter completely. I also got a personal one-on-one coaching from Sylvester when I was called for an interview."

"I have never felt confident and relaxed going to an interview as I did after going through all the possible interview questions and responses in the Job-getting Formula book with Sylvester. It is one-of-a-kind. Get your hands on the Job-getting Formula book and if you choose to take your job-getting skills even further, get on Sylvester's Coaching program as well, and you will not regret it."

"Once again, thank you Sylvester for the Job-getting Formula."

*---Stella Yufenyuy, Registered Nurse, San Jose, California, USA*

"We are introduced to yet another classic business dimension of thinking, different from the way we are used to. This book represents the quintessence of modern day job-getting techniques, certain to become a landmark classic for job seekers, compressed and superbly-organized into an easy read. Sylvester is neoteric. Rather than giving answers to questions like most books on job search, he is explaining a formula in an easy-to-understand language. With explanations, he uses his foresight to prepare and prevent job seekers from circumstances into which their hindsight would have fumbled them. *The Job Getting Formula* is a well structured, out-of-the-box thinking for job seekers as well as professionals seeking career changes, jobs-of-their-lives or high-paying jobs."

"*The Job Getting Formula* culminates to the summum bonum in job search. It is the best source of insight for job seekers to win in the face of a globally competitive job market. The author writes from personal experience, how his formula worked astonishingly and unflinchingly, revealing the unthinkable in the minds of hiring managers."

"If you want to awe hiring managers, boost the clarity of your job search, enhance confidence in your communication and land the job of your dreams… then before you set foot into an active search for a high-paying job, get your hands on *The Job Getting Formula.*"

*---Valery Elad, MBA Student, Albany, New York, USA.*

"This book could not have been written at any better time than now, when many economies are witnessing the highest unemployment figures since 2008. Around the major cities of the world today, a huge number of graduates roam the streets. With the impacts of the recent economic crisis still too fresh to be forgotten, finding appropriate jobs has become even more challenging and complex than ever before."

"Addressing this endemic unemployment problem requires innovative ways of searching and finding well-paying and satisfying jobs. This is what Sylvester Nkongho achieves exceptionally well in his thought-out and insightful piece, *The Job Getting Formula.* One of the major strengths of the book is its focus not only on the advertised jobs – the 'business as usual' job repository – but also on the most high paying but often unadvertised jobs."

"The book provides clear guidance on how to influence your prospective employer to create a position for you without necessarily advertising the job! On the basis of its innovation, simplicity, succinctness, and clarity, I am convinced that this book is certainly a must-read not only for job seekers out there but also for those, including me, who feel the time has come to move on and take up fresh challenges in life by taking on new jobs."

*--- Dr. Ingr. Henry Abanda,*

*Research Engineer, Oxford Institute for Sustainable Development, United Kingdom*

"The Job-Getting Formula is a well-written, simple, yet powerful book that details a five step system for an experienced worker to get a high paying job. Each step is a value added tool building from the previous step, and provides a practical sequence to take you from where you are right now to where you desire to go – getting a high paying job."

"The book puts into context the dire situation many individuals around the world find themselves in, which is difficulty in finding a high-paying job in an unpleasant economy. What separates this book from other books in a similar category is that it outlines a simple yet practical process of getting a high paying job. There is a lot of 'lip service' out there on how to find a job but yet unemployment rates are sky-rocketing through the roof."

"This book is an asset in that the process it details encourages a paradigm shift, which provides a strong financial foundation for your life, and sets you up for life. It is much more than just a short cut to getting a high-paying job, but rather it empowers you in a way that will keep you gravitated to many opportunities in life because of the change in the way you think or begin to think."

*--- Mandy Shemuvalula, Founder, Visionary & President, M'che World, Inc.*

"I am highly thrilled by this book and I tell you… It goes beyond all continental boundaries. I have been trying to help people who passively look for jobs and was wondering which books were easy to read and could be recommended to them. You have tied the bolts and knots so neatly. I was shaken and stirred to a new wavelength of reasoning when I had the great honor of reading through the "Job getting formula".

"This masterpiece offers a compelling instinct for job seekers whose complacency with petty achievements has no place today. The book gives an admirable reflex that will jerk anyone with big and bold career plans to give "fear of the unknown" a decent burial and to swing into vision without further delay."

*--- Clement Yuyun, Head of Corporate Banking, Union Bank of Cameroon, Plc.*

# The Job getting Formula

## DEDICATION

This Book is dedicated to the person who first taught me the power of faith in "driving" the impossible.

She showed me that where there's a will there's a way.

She gave me love and a complete education despite the many and almost insurmountable obstacles she went through, and in the process she taught me, as a role model, what I interpreted as, "GO the extra mile and FETCH what you want!"

Mummy **ELIZABETH AYUK**, May Your SOUL REST In ETERNAL PEACE and HAPPINESS!

# Disclaimer

This book contains the opinions and ideas of its author. It is intended, in good faith, to provide helpful and informative material on the subjects addressed. By *really* studying this book and applying the ideas and advice, you will not only be able to get the high-paying job you want, you will also acquire essential and lifelong job-getting skills.

Due to the fact that the results anyone can obtain from any information product is directly linked to their skill level, personal commitment or other personal circumstances, this book is not guaranteed or warranted to produce any *particular* results. It is my opinion that most people who purchase ANY "how to" or "improvement" product... including but not limited to this book, get little if any results. I believe this is because they don't take action, and they don't keep trying after hitting some inevitable roadblocks.

If you want to succeed, you need to have a good plan, a solid work ethic, and the ability to keep working toward your goals without quitting. If you simply keep buying "how to" information and never use it, you're wasting your time.

This book is sold with the understanding that neither the author nor the publisher is engaged in rendering legal, financial, accounting, or other professional advice or services outside the author's core competence. The reader should consult a competent legal, financial, accounting, or any other relevant professional before adopting any of the suggestions in this book or drawing inferences from it.

# The Job getting Formula

# CONTENTS

# The Job getting Formula

# *INTRODUCTION*

## The "Risky Road" And Nasty Struggles That Led To Discovering The Job-getting Formula™

Randy was yelling "HEY, HEY, HEY, BE CAREFUL! WE'LL DIE!" The car was swinging from left to right and right to left, as I was wrestling to keep it on course. And BANG! We bumped into the side gutter. That was the END.

But I was still alive, though I couldn't come out because the doors were stuck against the sides of the V-shape gutter. I hurried out through the driver's side window.

"Are you ok?" Randy asked as he forced his way out through the passenger's side window. I was happily surprised that he too was still alive. "Thank God no car was coming close!", Randy gratefully exclaimed. "Yes, that would have crushed us to death, especially as the car was dangling on the road," I confirmed.

Randy was my friend and colleague, with whom I was driving to work. Thank God, we both had our seat belts on and they saved us.

But I was like… "Here's my red old scrappy Toyota car trying to kill me. Not to think of the deep debt I had gotten into, with the bank, just to afford it. That debt was now part of the huge burden on my meager monthly salary."

I kept asking myself, "What if I died? Why was I speeding, in the first place?" Then a second thought argued, "I had to. I was late for work."

As it was the routine, on Monday mornings, after a short weekend of relief from my humdrum job, I had to get up from sleep at 4 am, with the help of the screaming noise of the alarm clock, leave my temptingly sexy wife in bed, then commute from the Atlantic Oceanside city of Limbe to work in the neighboring city of Douala. That morning, I was late... (Love-making got me exhausted and sleep was sweet. I also had a minor problem with the engine coolant pump of my old car that contributed to the lateness.)

From Mondays through Fridays, I stayed with a friend in the city where I worked to avoid the fatigue from getting up too early. I could not rent another house or live in a hotel – that was out of the question. My debt-laden salary could not afford me the luxury.

For several years, I had been avoiding the question of looking for another high-paying job elsewhere. I simply never wanted to repeat the same struggle I went through before getting my first job, after leaving school.

I wanted to grow within the company I was working for. So, I figured out that for me to become more valuable to my boss, my employer, and my industry, I would need to do some sort of Certification or MBA, which would enable me stand out from the huge crowd of job seekers. So I enrolled into the SPSM (Senior Professional in Supply Management) Certification, one of the world's leading online certifications in Purchasing and Supply Management.

I kept improving my work with the ideas I got from my certification course, while keeping my fingers crossed, hoping one day things would change – and I would get a promotion.

But to my exasperation, I found that my boss was rather playing company politics with my desire for a promotion – to get me to work even harder for her selfish benefits.

2

So, I immediately activated my "Plan B", and started looking for another higher paying job. Before then, all along I was told, finding a job while working is fairly easy.

But I was terribly surprised when, from dozens of résumés and cover letters I sent out for job openings – you won't believe it – I was NEVER called, not even for a single interview.

I suspected there was a problem with my résumé and cover letter. So I bought all the books I could lay my hands on that carried advice on how to write attention-grabbing résumés and cover letters and on how to ace interviews.

In the next bunch of résumés and cover letters I sent out, I included all the techniques I learned from my résumé writing courses.

Yet to my greatest dismay, nothing happened!

I NEVER landed a single interview.

It was almost certain to me that I had zero luck with picking up a better-paying job.

I was always depressed when I saw some of my colleagues landing high-paying jobs within the company and in other BIG Companies, because I knew most of them were not smarter than I was.

Every single day that passed got me more FRUSTRATED!

Not being able to find another job after searching for too long, I incurred some additional loans to start a small bar business to supplement the little leftover I had as salary.

But this bar business was doing more damage to my finances than good. I guess it was because I had no previous experience in managing a business, let alone that type of business that needed a rigorous follow up of every detail.

Things were now very tight financially for me at the end of every month, and it was really difficult to make ends meet.

My salary when I got that job, though at the time sounded like a good salary, was now insufficient to pay my debts and take care of my needs. And my financial obligations kept increasing.

I couldn't even pride myself on having a salary, because immediately as I received my meager monthly salary, I had to pay all the bills and at the end, nothing was left for me to live on. It was like you're working but you're not seeing where the money is going. What was coming in was far less than what was going out.

The only way for me to continue living after paying all my bills was to get into further debt.

I was afraid of the way things were going. And I said to myself, "If I continue living like this, I may never get out of debt, and I may never live the life I have always dreamed of – like riding in a bigger luxurious car, owning a personal home of my choice, sending my kids to college and preparing them a brighter future, and all other good things that come with a good life."

And you know… when you're working, people expect a lot from you financially, especially in family and social circles. Nothing is more humiliating than when you can't improve or maintain your financial status among friends and family, or keep to your financial obligations and promises with creditors.

As crazy as it might sound, I was asking myself, "How can I have a way of connecting directly with a serious hiring manager who is just looking for a serious worker like myself and who can just give me a call, saying, 'Come and start working with me tomorrow'."

I just wanted a way – a "formula", to get another high-paying job and get out of my financial mess – compounded by the pesky treatment I was receiving from my boss.

By this time, all the job hunting books and programs I had tried seemed to be lacking some vital ingredients to make them work. They just didn't feel right. So I had to look for a better way out. And for those who know me, I hardly give up on anything I set my mind on. So I vowed, 'I must figure out a way to get a higher-paying job'."

Then somewhere along the way, a thought suddenly hit me that I should contact some senior purchasing managers in other companies and ask them about the problems they were facing with purchasing, in order to really see whether I could be of any advice with the fresh knowledge I had acquired from my certification. In the back of my mind, I knew this was a strategy to create some "networking" so that I would be informed earlier enough of any job opportunities before they ever reached the public announcement stage.

While I was going through that process, a vacancy was opened in Diageo-Guinness, United Kingdom, the headquarters of the same multi-national company I was working for. It was the position of Purchasing Category Manager which reported to the Head of Purchasing for Africa – my boss' functional boss, whom I'll simply refer to as Andy. Luckily, I had developed a good relationship with Andy as well as other people from the UK team, from when we all first met in a workshop in Ghana.

So, I contacted one of the UK guys to figure out what was *really* required for the position. I didn't want to go by the job description alone, as that had always been the case with my past failures.

Due to my longtime interest in becoming a consultant one day, I had also once read from a book on *'marketing and selling consulting services'* that finding the underlying problems of a client is crucial for success in getting hired as a consultant. But as an employee, I had never considered applying that principle to my job search.

Following that principle, and with the information I got about what was really required of the position, I mustered courage and applied for the position.

To my awesome amazement, I received an email from Andy that he would be calling me for an interview the following Wednesday at 2 pm. I was blown away with excitement and ecstasy.

I prayed that my boss should not get to know what was happening before the interview. And as if God heard my prayers, she knew nothing that was going on. And on that blessed Wednesday morning, something miraculous happened. She complained that she could not work because she had an excruciating neck pain, and she went back home.

At 2 pm I went into the meeting room and my phone rang. It was Andy and he interviewed me at length. Then he told me he'd get back to me a couple of weeks later.

Three weeks later, my boss called me into the meeting room and told me that Andy requested that she ask me if I'd like to move to the UK for a 3 to 6 months probationary period to see if I could occupy the *Regional Purchasing Category Manager* position. I happily accepted, and my mind was swimming with joy while I listened to and watched her speak. She was struggling to hold a smile on her face, as if she was happy for me. In my mind, I was saying to her, "I got you…you've seen nothing from me yet… this is just the beginning." And I felt a deep satisfying feeling of revenge. Who said, "Success is the best revenge"? Nothing could be truer.

It's worth noting that this was a position requiring someone with eight years of experience in a similar or closely related role and promised to pay more than twice my salary plus great benefits. But I had less than six years working experience. And it was yet a combined experience as opposed to purchasing experience only. That's when it dawned on me, for the first time, that this "experience thing" doesn't really matter in the real world – especially when you know what the hiring manager really wants.

As I was rejoicing over the effectiveness of my newly found résumé, cover letter and interview "tricks", while arrangements were being made for me to move to London, I stumbled on the book *Think And Grow Rich* by Napoleon Hill. I read every page of it. It is one of the greatest books I have ever read on success.

Next was Bob Proctor's *You Were Born Rich*, then the movie 'The Secret' and a whole lot of personal development books, audio and video programs. I also watched YouTube videos, and bought and studied books and home study courses from the world's greatest teachers like John Assaraf, Jack Canfield, Brian Tracy, Mark Victor Hansen, Les Brown, Jim Rohn, Zig Zigglar, Tony Robbins, Robert Kiyosaki and a few others.

As I was studying these things, all of a sudden my belief about myself changed and a new world of awareness opened up to me. My self-confidence increased dramatically and I quickly realized that my job-getting techniques were so powerful that I could use them at any time to get whatever high-paying job I wanted. The only thing for me to figure out before writing my résumé and cover letter was "What's in the mind of the hiring manager or hiring decision maker?". I quickly realized that without this information, the rest is complete waste of time and effort (only extreme luck can get you called for an interview if you don't have this key information).

With this evolved awareness and the confidence in my job-getting techniques, I did one of the craziest things in the eyes of everybody who ever knew me!

To the surprise of everyone, I resigned from my job and created my own Advice, Consulting, Coaching and Training business. I knew deep within that I had "cracked the code" of how to get a high-paying job.

(I remember my boss asking… "What about the promotion I have been negotiating for you…, and the assignment to the UK?" To which, I didn't respond, but rather I stared at her with a look that meant, "To the abyss of HELL with all that CRAP!")

Instead of moving to another job that would give me a bit more money but less time and freedom to enjoy it, I decided that I would use the same techniques to get jobs with companies where I could be an independent consultant and start my own consulting business.

With my newly found job-getting techniques, I could get new business for myself in the form of consulting jobs. I KNEW, without any doubt that that was the ULTIMATE way to freedom.

But I also knew that if the worst came to worst and things got very bad on the business side (especially with my limited business experience at the time), I could still look for another job with my easy job-getting techniques.

And really… a couple of months later, it got really tough with my business.

I was still in business but new consulting work was coming in very slowly. After doing one job, it would take months to get another. In fact, I was making the same big mistake many people make while they have a good "permanent" job. They never think about tomorrow or that one day things might get rough.

That is… instead of starting to look for another consulting job immediately after having a new one, I would wait until the job I had in hand expired before I started looking for another one. Instead of prospecting about ten different companies in a row so that I would always have something in the pipeline to jump to after my current assignment expires, I stayed contented with the job I had and was simply surprised when the job finally got to an end. I was operating with a typical employee mindset, instead of that of an independent business owner.

And you know, contrary to a "permanent" job (I put permanent in quotes because such a job doesn't exist in reality…but anyway, that aside…), there is no fixed salary when you are working only on assignment contracts as a consultant.

As you might have guessed, even the bar business that I created and named "Futuris" came crashing down as well. Futuris never saw the future.

So, it got to a point where I was supposed to look for another "permanent" job alongside my consulting business, in order to take care of some fixed monthly bills and to pay my accrued debts.

For me it was rather simple. I followed the same information-getting process as before to figure out *exactly* what problem the hiring manager really wanted to solve. But this time, from my additional experience as a consultant, I sent out a few interview-getting résumés and cover letters and a *special document* (that I will reveal later) to well targeted, *unadvertised* positions. A couple of weeks later, I was called for an interview.

This one really surprised me: I was given the job the same day on the spot… and it was about double the salary of my previous job.

Once again, in the real world, my job-getting techniques were tried, tested and proven to work. This rang a bell for me to see how to tighten "the nuts and bolts" and put this into a formula or system that anyone could use. I knew there were millions of people out there who needed help and will be glad to have this type of information.

And so, I went to work and created what is now known as the job-getting formula for getting a high-paying job. This is the formula that is described in the pages of this book, in 5 simple steps.

But before we dive into the 5 steps, let's get clear on what a high-paying job is and what it can do for you.

Generally, a high-paying job is one that offers you more purchasing power.

In fact, a high-paying job is the type of job that offers you most of the "good things in life", like:

- Getting out of debt,

- Getting a luxury car - the type that gets you admired by friends and that you'd be proud of,

- Keeping your love relationship or marriage in harmony,

- Getting a beautiful house of your choice,

- Extra money for personal or family vacation,

- Free or company-paid travel to great places all over the world,

- Free housing,

- Health insurance coverage,

- Enough money to save on "special projects",

- Enough money to spend on weekends, on social life, and "special outings",

- Enough money for children's schooling,

- Enough money for maintaining a healthy lifestyle,

- And anything in between.

All these are what I call the "lifestyle benefits" of a high-paying job.

And these types of benefits are hard, if not impossible, to get without a high-paying job.

But here is the problem: It will be extremely difficult to get a high-paying job if you follow the traditional job hunting approach – especially with the huge competition for jobs out there.

So why is it so? And what is the traditional approach?

The traditional approach is chasing after jobs that are advertized to the public. These are jobs that attract hundreds and even thousands of applicants with the same qualifications, skills and experience, as yours.

With advertized jobs, most applicants have the job requirements and they can simply adjust their résumé to match the job. This also makes it even more competitive.

And the result? Your chances of being selected for interviews are reduced… CONSIDERABLY reduced!

Now, remember the old law of supply and demand?

When the competition goes up, the price goes down. And so does the salary for a highly competitive, openly-advertised job. Which implies, even if you're selected for a highly competitive position, the final offer may not come up to an exciting high-paying package.

So, what should you do?

It's simple.

You should target jobs that have these two characteristics:

1.   The job is known by YOU ALONE.

2.   Nobody is as WILLING and READY to fill the job as you are.

This approach would really lower the competition... almost to zero. And it will offer you high chances of negotiating a lucrative high-paying package.

I know you are asking, "How is getting this type of job possible?"

Well, for you to really understand that this is very possible and easy, let's look at how jobs are created in the real world.

You see, when a company or an employer has a problem to solve, they go looking for people who have the skills to solve that problem. And when they find someone with those skills, they then offer them the job. Then they give a title or a name for that position.

If after some time, the person holding that position leaves the company for whatever reason, the company would then go put out an ad to the public describing the title and requirements of the vacancy.

At this point, the company knows exactly what they are searching for, because they've filled that position before and know what skills are necessary to do the job.

And they also know what salary they have paid in the past for that position and what they can pay in the future to a person applying for that type of position. (And even more advantageous for the company is the fact that many people will apply and compete for the position, thereby allowing for an even lower salary.)

Here's an example. Let's say a prestigious company is looking for someone to do their internet marketing, because they have realized that there's a HUGE opportunity to make millions by marketing online.

They'll then go looking for somebody who is good and experienced with marketing on the internet. When they get such a person, they'll then create a high-paying job for that person, with a title such as "Online Marketing Manager" or "Internet Marketing Officer", or anything of that sort.

As you can see, the name doesn't really matter as much as compared to what the person is called to do.

When other people notice that companies of that nature as well as their competitors are now looking for internet marketing specialists for a high pay, people start specializing and searching for jobs in that area. After a while that particular job title becomes saturated in the market.

Now let's say, the very first person who was recruited for the position of "Internet Marketing Officer" was previously working for her former company as marketing manager, in charge of every other aspect of marketing, but had some experience or knowledge in internet marketing as a new medium of marketing. And when she found, through a friend or a connection, or however, that a prestigious company was looking for someone with internet marketing experience, she contacted the company and presented her application. At the time, that person happened to be the only one available among the few people with that type of experience to fill that pressing need.

And therefore, they were offered a high-paying position, with "cool" benefits, to handle internet marketing for that prestigious company.

For you to really understand what I am saying… here are other examples of how people find high-paying jobs that pay BIG MONEY.

- A *"Journalist"* of ABC-TV becomes the *"Corporate Communication Director"* of a renowned multinational Company for thrice her salary.

- A young *"Practicing Lawyer"* becomes the *"Chief Legal Consultant"* of a fast growing start-up business that pays twice as much.

- A *"Storekeeper"* of a supermarket or grocery store becomes the *"Fulfillment manager"* of a fast-growing online information products business for a much higher salary.

- And the list goes on and on.

As I've just described, after a job position and title is well known in the job market, it becomes very competitive in the long run. And the reason for this is obvious: Many people are hunting for it. And it becomes difficult for such a position to stay at a high salary.

But the sad fact is that, 99 out of every 100 people are still searching for a high-paying job using this highly competitive approach.

Now, don't get me wrong. If you are looking for any type of job, that would pay a *little bit* more than your current job, then you can follow this old approach.

But if you do your thinking well, you'd find that, for this old approach to even work, the advertised job must really match your qualification. I mean the type of vacancy for which you are 100% sure your qualification and experience are unique and would make you stand out as the favorite candidate.

But again, finding a high-paying job in this way is one of the things that stop many people from EVER getting it in the first place.

I hear it all the time...

*"I'm having trouble getting a high-paying job, with the type of benefits I want."*

*"Jobs in my area of specialty don't pay well."*

But what is sad is that, I also hear most employers saying that they have job opportunities but they can't find people with the right skills and qualifications to fill them.

The "problem" with these problems is simple.

In some cases, it's a problem of a total lack of skills in the job market. In other cases, it has to do with the *inability* of people to transfer or adapt their skills, or *communicate correctly* about newly acquired skills.

But this is what it all boils down to:

If you cannot find and target an emerging problem faced by a given company or industry and adapt or position your skills, knowledge and experience to offer a unique solution to it, then you'd HARDLY get a high-paying job…

…At least, the kind that will help you get out of debt, enable you get a luxury car, a decent home, job satisfaction, and everything in between.

But if you're really serious about getting a high-paying job with "cool" benefits that match your lifestyle, then you MUST change the way you look for it.

If you look at the examples I have given you, you'd realize that, a high-paying job isn't something that you sit and wait for, unless you are counting on dumb luck alone – in which case you're not different from a typical gambler or lottery player. (I guess you don't want to keep your fingers "crossed" as I did for far too long only to my greatest desperation that nothing was changing or was ever going to change, if I didn't take action.)

A high-paying job is rather something you MUST *carefully* search for. It is something that must be *found*. A high-paying job must be *discovered, uncovered* and *"solved",* just like a miner (or gold digger) must dig, uncover a gold mine and extract the gold out of it.

The 3 things you must do to get a high-income job with great lifestyle benefits and advantages are:

1.  Find a need or problem that an employer or industry is facing.

2.  Improve on your existing skills or develop new skills to fit into the solution of the employer's problem.

3.  Position and communicate your skills, knowledge and experience to the employer in a way that makes you unique and "fit" to solve the employer's problem.

In essence, getting a high-paying job is about thinking like the employer. That is what the Job-getting formula is all about.

The Job-getting Formula™ is a unique approach to finding and getting a high-paying job.

It focuses on your strengths and how you can leverage them in relation to all the opportunities available for you in the *high-demand skills* market where more than 80% of the high-paying jobs are found, but ignored by almost 99% of job seekers.

It ensures that you search for and discover real problems faced by employers, as timely as they emerge. Then you bring all your valuable skills, knowledge, experience, and qualifications to *align* with the solutions to those problems.

Next, you "package" (in the form of an interview-getting résumé, interview-getting cover letter and a special marketing document I will reveal to you later) and sell your skills, knowledge, experience, and qualifications in the most compelling manner to employers who are in desperate need of them…

…So that you can get the high-paying job that will make others envy you, free you from debt and financial stress, fit your lifestyle in a unique way, and offer you all the exciting benefits you REALLY WANT.

The Job-getting Formula has been designed to offer you UNIQUE, SIMPLE and INDEPTH answers to all your *big questions* about employers and getting a high-paying job.

It simplifies everything about getting a high-paying job into practical step-by-step answers to 5 KEY questions, which are ALWAYS on the mind of the prospective Employer or their hiring managers and hiring decision makers. These are the questions that drive their hiring decisions when looking for someone to solve a specific business problem.

Solving a business problem boils down to filling a job position.

And here are the 5 BIG QUESTIONS employers use to assess a candidate's FITNESS for a job position:

1. **Big Question 1:** Are you PASSIONATE and WILLING to fit into the high-paying job, more than any other candidate?

2. **Big Question 2:** Do you know the prospective employer's PROBLEMS and DESIRES, better than any other candidate?

3. **Big Question 3:** Can you DELIVER RESULTS, despite on-the-job challenges, better than any other candidate?

4. **Big Question 4:** Can you CONTACT the employer and let them know you can deliver results, better than any other candidate?

5. **Big Question 5:** Can you PROVE, in an interview, that you are fit for the job, better than any other candidate?

The degree of success with which you can *practically* answer ALL FIVE questions determines your chances of getting the Job.

In other words, if you can answer <u>YES with PROOF</u> to all 5 questions, more than any other candidate for a given high-paying job position, then you are guaranteed to get the job.

And therefore the Formula:

**(Q1 = YES) + (Q2 = YES) + (Q3 = YES) + (Q4 = YES) + (Q5 = YES) = JOB**

This is the Job-getting Formula!

It's simple… right?

But trust me, it is more powerful than you imagine.

As you'll soon realize, my intention with this book is to make it the ULTIMATE advice book to teach you how to influence hiring managers *directly*… in a way that makes them literally create a high-paying job for you, where there was supposed to be none… so that… you can live the great lifestyle you really want.

Not only did it take me YEARS to learn, figure out, and apply all of this stuff in the first place, but it also took me literally THOUSANDS of hours of my time to put this particular book together.

I really designed this "thing" from start to finish, for it to be the simplest and absolute best advice available in the world on how to influence hiring managers and hiring decision-makers to give you the high-paying job you really want. NO Kidding!

At this point you may ask: Does it mean that if someone violates any of the variables or does not score a "Yes" with any of the 5 job-getting formula questions, they cannot get the Job?

The answer is NO.

In such a case, they can get the job only through EXTREME LUCK – mostly due to a mis-hire on the part of the employer or its hiring decision makers. And that can lead to short or long-term negative consequences for the employer's company.

According to the book *"Top Grading"* by Brad Smart, a company could lose 10 to 12 times an employee's annual salary following a mis-hire.

Today, due to the difficult and changing economic situation, employers are tightening their recruitment processes to ensure that only the best candidates are hired.

That is why the hiring process today is generally one where a HUGE focus is placed on *screening* and *disqualifying* candidates rather than *selecting and including* them.

As you must have realized, the Human Resource departments of most companies and other recruiting agencies spend more time looking for ways to *screen out* candidates who do not respect the Job-getting Formula (or a similar version of it) in order to minimize the risk of miss-hires.

In the process, most HR and Recruiting firms have become exclusion experts, with often roughly-developed screening processes, which most of the time eliminate even candidates who are competent for the job but who DO NOT UNDERSTAND THE RULES OF THE HIRING PROCESS AND HOW TO CONQUER IT.

## 5 BIG Reasons Why Most People Fail To Get the High-paying Jobs They Want… And How To Avoid Making The Same Mistakes

1. **Reason #1:** Employers are looking for passionate and service-dedicated A-players who are driven to deliver results, and who would do anything creative and unconventional to "crack" high-demand skill opportunities and get the jobs they are passionate about. Most job seekers lack the passion, drive and energy for the jobs they go after, thereby violating Big Question 1 of the Job-getting Formula.

   In Step 1 of this book, you'll learn the secret mindset and winning habits that will offer you "insurance" against failure in getting the high-paying job you want.

2. **Reason #2:** Most people DO NOT take time to investigate the problem of the prospective employer before applying for the job – they therefore send out generic résumés and cover letters, which confirm that they do not have a clue about the employer's problems. Again, violating Big Question 2 of the Job-getting Formula.

   In Step 2 of this book, you'll learn what I call the "Gold Digger's Approach" for figuring out the *exact* problem, for which an employer is willing to pay you, as high as possible, to solve.

3. **Reason #3:** Most job seekers send out weak and mediocre résumés and cover letters that DO NOT market and sell their in-demand skills and accomplishments to the employer – instead, these portray them as incompetent "paycheck mongers" who can't deliver results. This violates Big Question 3 of the Job-getting Formula.

In Step 3 of this book, you'll learn how to combine over 12 Rules of Influence and other "bad-ass" techniques to FORCE a hiring manager (or hiring decision maker) to call you for an interview.

4. **Reason #4:** Most job seekers, despite great skills, experience and qualifications, may fall short of the courage (fear of rejection), skills, and techniques of *directly* contacting informants, in order to rip off vital information regarding problems faced by employers, on one hand; and meet hiring managers to sell their in-demand skills, on the other hand. This violates Big Question 4.

In Step 4 of this book, I will show you how to contact a hiring manager, head of department or hiring decision maker… in a way that makes them see you as competent, confident and "mature" for the high-paying job you want.

5. **Reason #5:** Most job seekers, who succeed to get to the interview stage, fail to prove their worth as marketed and sold by their résumé and cover letter. This is because they lack insider knowledge about the interviewing techniques and psychology used by recruiters, hiring managers and hiring decision makers for judging candidates. This directly violates Big Question 5, and stops them from passing an interview and getting a high-paying job that offers the great lifestyle benefits they want.

In Step 5 of this book, I will reveal over 190 toughest interview questions as well as the psychology, rules, formulas and techniques for answering them.

The rest of this book deals with the details of each Step (or BIG Question) of the Job-getting Formula. You will discover simple, never-before revealed secrets you never could fathom on your own. I will walk you step-by-step in each one of the killer techniques as we move on.

Let's dive in…

# The Job getting Formula

## STEP 1

## Are You PASSIONATE And WILLING To "Fit" Into The High-Paying Job, More Than Any Other Candidate? (Here's Your "Insurance" Against Failure)

Eric Schmidt, Executive Chairman of Google, was once asked what they look for when hiring people to work for their company. He said, the two essential qualities they look for in candidates are:

1. *Personal drive* and *passion.*

2. *A track record of getting things done.*

He went on to say that the Stars, the "A players", or the real Winners don't work for money. They work for impact.

One of the most important things employers look for in job seekers is the passion and willingness to do the job.

In this Step of the formula, we'll be focusing on passion, drive and willingness to fit into a particular high-paying job. We'll see *why* and *how* these qualities can help you get the high-paying job you want.

We'll also look at some of the *winning habits* that will help improve your track record of achievements (or getting things done, as Eric Schmidt puts it).

It's worth noting that, without passion, there will be no drive or willingness to do a particular job.

21

The big question therefore is...

How do you know that a particular high-paying job fits your passion? Or, how do you know that you have passion for a certain type of job?

So, we want to study what creates passion and how one can assess their passion for a job... because, if someone happens to find his or herself in a job that he/she does not feel driven or passionate about, they can hardly excel at it.

No matter how high the job pays, if there is no passion and willingness to "fit" into it, there can hardly be great performance and personal fulfillment.

Most employers know this truth and therefore, they will do everything possible to determine if a candidate is passionate and willing to fit into a particular job.

That brings us to the question of... what does the word passion itself mean? What do we mean by someone feeling passion for something?

Well, the word *passion* itself is a very broad word.

A person may be passionate positively or negatively about anything – e.g. passionate about a loved one, sports, food, children, family, animals, etc.

The dictionary defines passion as *any powerful or compelling emotion or feeling, as love or hate, for someone or something.*

But let's try to focus on passion as it relates to a job and let's talk about what makes someone feel passion for a job.

Based on my research and my own personal experience, here is the simplest definition I can give you about passion with regards to a job:

*Passion for a job is a powerful and compelling inner drive and emotion we have for doing something (a job) that contributes positively to the lives of others and that rewards us in a way that enables us to enjoy most of our other passions.*

Here are some examples:

- If you are passionate about home and family life, you might not be passionate about getting a job that keeps you away from your family, even if the job promises to pay high enough.

- If you are passionate about animals, travel and adventure, then you are very likely to be passionate about getting a high-paying job that gets you into constant travel and discovery of new animals and places, e.g. a wildlife researcher.

- If you are naturally intuitive and a bit introverted, and you are passionate about ideas and concepts, then you might like to get a high-paying job that offers you the luxury to work creatively in "ideas space" and behind-the-scenes to develop concepts that would help others, e.g. software designer, architect, psychologist, writer, teacher, etc.

- If you are someone who is deeply passionate about cars, you are very likely to be passionate about working for a car sales business as salesman or sales agent, so you'd have the luxury to touch, feel and test-drive a wide variety of cars. You'd also have the exciting opportunity to tell customers and friends about the wonderful features that are available in different models of cars.

  On top of your passion for cars, if you also like interacting with less familiar people like car customers, then you'll really be passionate and willing to do everything to get a car salesman job.

I often get the question from people: "How can I find passion in a job that I might not completely like but that promises to pay high enough?"

To answer that question, let's consider the car example again, but this time differently:

Let's say you love cars but you do not like to sell or interact face-to-face with new and unfamiliar people. And that you happen to be going after a lucrative "car sales agent" job. Let's say you are also afraid of rejection from unfamiliar people when trying to sell them something.

In that case, you'd need to develop a passion and willingness for selling and overcoming rejection first, before you can be completely passionate and driven about getting a car salesman job.

What this tells us is that… PASSION CAN BE DEVELOPED.

In other words, it's from the pursuit of passion that more passion comes. And that also means… the high-paying job you want might not be your complete passion *initially*, but might serve as a stepping stone to your passion.

You can develop passion for something, by changing the way you think about it.

Here's an example:

Before starting to write this 'Step 1' of the book, I was just coming from a long morning jogging – some sort of a mini marathon.

I had never covered such a jogging distance in the past – never before, in any of my morning exercising. But that morning, something shifted in my head.

The way I used to think about exercising had just changed drastically… And so was the drastic difference between the distance I used to cover and the one I covered that morning.

I used to think that exercising was boring (I think it was because I wasn't seeing immediate results of the amount of pounds lost from my efforts) – and that it was all about the difficult process of losing weight. Of course, part of exercising is about weight loss. But that way of looking at exercising did not motivate me to love and do more of it.

Initially, when I woke up that morning feeling less energy in my body, I recalled that, usually after exercising, I often feel much more energy in my body.

That morning, while I was procrastinating on whether to go exercise or not, something suddenly clicked inside my head. I had this idea to go do some exercise as a means to gain some energy.

And behold, following that decision, I did a distance that was thrice longer than any other I had ever done… simply because, I went for *the energy* and not for *losing weight* – even though I knew weight loss was an obvious side benefit.

Every extra step I took running ahead felt as if it was adding more energy to my body. And so, I couldn't afford to stop going, until I felt I had enough energy to take me through that entire day.

As Dr. Wayne Dyer said, *"When you change the way you look at something, the thing you look at changes."* And I found this statement to be 100% true.

Previously, when I went out for workouts (or exercising), it really felt boring. I usually counted how much distance I had covered, how many pushups I had made or how many times I had lifted a certain weight. And if I thought I had done enough, which was hardly enough in reality, I stopped immediately.

But when I changed my focus and my thinking from that of "losing weight" and "how many times I have done a particular type of workout routine"… to that of "gaining energy"… EVERYTHING changed!

I was now motivated, because I knew I had a benefit to gain. The payoff was the energy I gained, to carry out my business activities, which I am really passionate about and which is my number one passion.

Without this energy, I would be inefficient in performing my passion, which is writing this book, creating the video trainings, and doing job-getting advice and coaching.

But by changing my attitude towards exercising, which I wasn't initially passionate about, I managed to increase my performance and my passion for both my business and exercising.

So what's the moral of my story?

Simple.

The way you look at the high-paying job you really want will seriously affect your attitude and the amount of effort you'd be *willing* to invest in order to get it.

In other words, your *passion* for any job also depends on the way you think about the job and all other aspects and circumstances surrounding it.

Your passion also depends on your core values, beliefs and lifestyle.

We humans come into this life with our own unique "wiring" and natural preferences about life and things, in general. We have our own perspective of how the world around us is, or is supposed to be.

And we feel more comfortable with things that are consistent with that perspective. And we tend to have a "negative take" on things that do not match our perspective.

While there are certain types of jobs that match our natural preferences, there are others that do not.

For example, depending on your personality type, you might *like* or *hate* the following:

- A high-paying job that gets you constantly travelling to new places, staying away from home several days a week and meeting new and less familiar people like customers, suppliers, colleagues, etc., without enough time to spend with family or friends, e.g. a business development manager, news reporter, flight attendant, management consultant, etc.

- A job that demands you to use only pre-established skills without the opportunity to learn new skills, or requires you to follow step-by-step routine instructions with a *very restricted* "personal touch" of choice, analysis, judgment, decision or creativity, e.g. a machine room attendant, waiter/waitress, receptionist, etc.

- A high-paying job that demands your creativity, judgment, analysis, and intuition to work alone, "behind-the-scenes" and figure things out by yourself, but without having to interact with new and less familiar people like customers, suppliers, etc., e.g. a researcher, software designer, graphic designer, writer, etc.

So, like these examples, what would you do if you found an opportunity for a high-paying job that had some aspects that you didn't like?

Will you be WILLING to develop PASSION for learning and loving some of the other aspects of the job that you don't like... by perhaps changing the way you think about it? What about putting in all the necessary efforts it takes to even get the high-paying job in the first place?

Will you be able to maintain a high level of energy, resilience, desire and enthusiasm to go after the high-paying job, with all the hassle (e.g. multiple rejections) until you get it?

Will you be willing to follow all the steps and advice I'll be teaching you in this Job-getting Formula book to finally "land" the high-income job you really want?

From my experience and research of studying winners and losers, I have found that all winners – including those I call the "job-getters" – have an extraordinary bulldog drive and willingness to achieve their goals.

They have a passion as many other people do. But their passion is so strong that they are willing to endure EVERYTHING it takes to get what they want. And I have found that, what makes their passion so strong is the promises that are wrapped up in their vision of the future.

For example, if a winner is pursuing the goal of a high-paying job... generally, what he or she has is this so-called tendency to dream of *already* living the life that is only possible if they have that high-paying job. The bigger the promise of a good life in their visualized future the bigger the price they are willing to pay. They are big practical dreamers, who dream of a bright future backed by a high-paying job, and then take consistent and persistent action to manifest that future.

This bulldog willingness of winners is rooted in 12 common winning habits they all practice, to make sure they achieve their goals, which make them completely different from losers. This set of 12 Secret Habits is like their insurance against failure.

And in the same way, the absence of these habits in the lives of many people have caused them to be losers, no matter how strong their passion was initially.

So, NO MATTER HOW STRONG OUR PASSION IS, for a given high-paying job, WE RISK NOT GETTING IT if we don't practice most or all of these 12 habits... even if we have all the secrets, tools and advice I will be sharing with you in this book.

I call them the *12 Habit Pillars*. And I described each of them, in detail, in my book entitled:

**Think Rich or Die Poor**: *"Why Are Winners Always Attracting Riches... And Which 12 Secret Habits You MUST Develop If You Ever Want To Become A Winner"*

Here is a brief summary of these habits and how they can be applied to help you get the high-paying job you want.

1. **Habit # 01 - Partnering with God (or Serving Humanity).**

   This is the habit of finding and living by a higher purpose, life passion, or worthy ideal. You can look at it as your ultimate goal to contribute to the lives of others and receive a reward in return. That's fulfilling God's purpose, or a higher purpose, towards service for you and others.

   For example, let's say you want to end up having your own business... or you want to create a charity foundation... or you want to contribute to the development of your town or community… or create a movement to help empower the underprivileged… and the list continues…

Whatever it is, your purpose is something BIG and EXCITING. It is your ultimate goal in life.

If the high-paying job you're looking for is a step towards achieving your purpose, then you'd do EVERYTHING to get it. And the hiring manager will sense it. They'll know that you're passionate to have the job more than anyone else. And that will only contribute to getting you the job.

## 2. Habit # 02 – Singleness of Purpose.

This is the habit of sticking to one unique ultimate purpose by continuously setting and achieving goals that will progressively lead you to that purpose.

If the high-paying job you're looking for is one of the goals you must achieve in order to get to your unique and compelling purpose, and since you'd do everything to remain on course through the habit of singleness of purpose, then you'd do everything to get that particular high-paying job.

So my question for you is this:

What is your DEFINITE (or single) purpose in life? Or, what do you want to start and *keep doing* 5 years from now going forward, for the rest of your life? (Notice the emphasis on the words "*keep doing*")

To answer this important question, here are the steps to follow:

1. Decide what your major purpose in life shall be.

2. Get a brand new notebook.

3. Write out a clear concise statement of this purpose.

4.  Write down a plan or plans through which you intend to achieve your purpose. (Note: This plan should be in the form of a series of steps of the things that *must happen* – even if you do not know how they'll happen – for your purpose to be achieved).

5.  Include as part of this plan or plans the high-paying job you want as one of the things that *must happen* for you to achieve your life's purpose.

## 3. Habit # 03 – Daily Goal Setting and Visualizing.

It is our daily activities that sum up to achieving our goals.

In other words, you must achieve your daily goals if you want to achieve your monthly or yearly goals.

Just having a purpose and goals on paper or in your mind without focusing your attention on them on a daily basis will not help you in any way.

You must form the habit of visualizing the results or outcome of your goals while setting and taking daily action steps to move them to realization.

You'd need to equally do this daily visualizing, daily-activities setting (or planning) and taking action with your job-getting goal in order to achieve it.

When you visualize and see yourself already living the life that comes with the high-paying job you want, it increases your desire, generates positive energy and motivates you to take action. And the actions you take, following the techniques described in this book, will get you the high-paying job you want.

A burning desire – generated through daily visualization of your "ideal" high-paying job – is like the fuel that MUST burn to produce the energy necessary to drive you to action and accomplishment. Without this type of desire, there will be no fuel to take you along, even if you have the road map of job-getting techniques described in this book.

The bigger the promise in your visualization, the bigger the price you'll be willing to pay.

Failure to visualize your goals will get you distracted and kill your desire. And NO DESIRE means NO ENERGY to go after the high-paying job you really want. Period!

When you don't have fuel, there's no other way about it – except you "tow" yourself up, just like towing a heavy car – which is synonymous to struggle, boredom, fatigue, feeling as if you are giving in too much hard effort, becoming discouraged, etc.

Whereas, with fuel or a burning desire, you don't even feel like you're working. You step into the flow of energy from within and you enjoy the ride, effortlessly.

So, here's what to do:

1. Read the statement of definite purpose you wrote in your notebook every morning when you wake up from sleep and every night before falling asleep.

2. Close your eyes and visualize with *intense emotion* how your life would be if you achieved the high-paying job you want, as being a major step on the path to your life's purpose.

3. Meditate or think deeply about the realization of your plan.

4. Write down in your notebook any idea that "pops" out of your mind, as you do your thinking or meditation.

5. Write down in your notebook three things or actions you'll do during the day that will move you a step towards getting the high-paying job you want.

6.  Do the 3 things you planned doing.

## 4. Habit # 04 – Requesting and Receiving Divine Guidance.

Going after a high-paying job is like trying to lose weight. Often, at the start, the results are slow, no matter the efforts.

When times are hard, such as when things are moving slower than you expected, you'll need to go into some form of retreat, introspection, meditation or prayer to find wisdom, calm down your doubts, fears and worries and regain focus.

You'd have to look for a quiet place to think through all your strategies, make necessary corrections and adjustments, and listen to your voice of instinct and intuition for divine guidance. That's the only moment you'd discover most of the little errors you made along the way and how to correct them the next time.

That's why Blaise Pascal, the great French philosopher and scientist said, "All man's miseries derive from not being able to sit quietly in a room alone."

## 5. Habit # 05 – Continuous Goal-oriented Learning.

Winners always learn what it takes to achieve their goals.

Your goal here is the high-paying, success-sized-salary job you want.

You'll have to form the habit of learning all the job-getting techniques in this book. You'll have to learn additional skills required to do the job and deliver results.

You can learn on the job, attend seminars, or take part time and online courses as required for the job.

For example, consultants and experts don't know everything. But they are considered by companies and their customers to be the "know-it-alls." The strength of consultants and experts is that they find out what their customers want and do everything to learn and provide it to them. They are always learning.

You have to develop the habit of continuous goal-oriented learning, in order to be able to deliver the results of the high-paying job you want.

Also, form the habit of reading books, listening to audio or watching video trainings *more than once*.

My coach, Bob Proctor, told me how he has been reading the "Think and Grow Rich" book since 1961, when he was 26 years old. Today, he's 76 and he's still reading the same book for 50 years. I started reading that book since I was 32, and I have never stopped. I hardly read any *good* book only once, because repetition is the first law of learning.

Often, it's not about reading an entire book all over. It's about re-reading parts of it, and using it for reference. And each time you do, your consciousness evolves. You see the same ideas in a new light.

So read this book several times. Use it as a reference guide. You'll be glad you did. If you don't, you won't even know why you're not getting ahead with getting the high-paying job you want, as well as the good life that comes with it. That's how you demonstrate your willingness to fit into the big salary job you want. And eventually, you'll get it and your life will never be the same again.

## 6.  Habit # 06 – Masterminding and Cooperating.

You'll need to work in collaboration with other people, especially those in your network, in order to succeed.

Without real collaboration and masterminding, it would be pretty difficult to get the help of others, which might be critical to your success in getting a job that really pays big money.

You'll also need to avoid people who discourage you from "thinking big" and pursuing your job-getting goals. If you don't, they'll kill your desire and "drain out" your fuel.

Look for people who encourage you, people who think big as you do. They'll turbo-charge your desire and energy like a rocket heading for the moon.

7. **Habit # 07 – Developing Multiple Sources of Income.**

This habit is a more advanced one, reserved for those who want to use their future high-paying jobs as a means of increasing their income by developing multiple streams of income.

It becomes relevant after you've got your high-paying job, which will then offer you extra income to build income-generating assets.

You might be saying... what's the need for other sources of income when I already have a high-paying job?

Guess what? You can equally increase your cash flow by using your high-paying job to develop other sources of passive income, which do not necessarily need your presence.

Such sources of passive income include, but are not limited to: investing in stocks and business ventures, getting involved in network marketing, sharing your experience and expertise in the form of a book, investing in real estate rental property (a sophisticated phrase for buying or building a house and leasing it out for rent), etc. These are just a few of the cash flow assets you can establish for continuous passive income.

This habit will only put extra money in your pocket and make you richer.

This is the secret to wealth. Take it as a bonus!

8. **Habit # 08 – Turning Failure Into Opportunity (Learning from Failure).**

In the course of applying the job-getting techniques in this book, everything you'll experience will be a learning experience.

If you do take a certain action and you don't get the exact results you expected, all you have to do is tweak your action a little bit and give it another try.

Winners are always inspired by failure and take temporary failure as valuable feedback to correct their actions.

It may be that you applied a particular technique but not as *exactly* as it is supposed to be done. Then when you get a near-miss result, instead of beating yourself up, take time to review and make corrections for the next time.

As Napoleon Hill said in his classic success book, *Think and Grow Rich*, "Before success comes in any person's life, he/she is sure to meet with much temporary defeat, and, perhaps, some failure. When defeat overtakes a person, the easiest and most logical thing to do is to QUIT. That is exactly what the majority of people do."

He went on to say… "Wherever men and women accumulate great riches, you may be sure they first acquired PERSISTENCE. Broadway (*the New York commercial theater, the amusement world and playground of success and fame*) will give any beggar a cup of coffee and a sandwich, but it demands PERSISTENCE of those who go after the big stakes."

I hope you'll not be like the majority of men and women who quit long before success ever comes their way. That's why they don't get high-paying jobs (the big stakes). They get only low or average-paying jobs (a cup of coffee and a sandwich).

The GREAT news is that, instead of taking several YEARS of research, reading, and trying crazy stuff that doesn't work (like I did), you can get the benefits of my "banging my head against the wall" research and experience... and go straight to getting the high-paying job you want, using the formulas in this book.

Learn from my failures and what I have discovered that works. BUT again, always remember...WINNERS NEVER QUIT AND QUITTERS NEVER WIN!

## 9. Habit # 09 – Rich Thinking and Decision Making

Your thinking and decision-making is critical to your success.

Winners make decisions right where they are with what they've got. They don't procrastinate.

Winners make their own decisions while losers suffer from "Approval Addiction" and indecision.

Unless you make a FIRM COMMITMENT to yourself that you'll get the high-paying job you really want, nothing significant will happen, despite all the great secrets and techniques you'll learn in this book. A firm commitment is a decision.

Winners know nothing happens by chance – all is based on Cause and Effect, and that they are a key agent of the cause. Losers believe most of life is about luck and that they are victims of circumstances.

So, at this stage, the WISEST thing for you to do is to make a decision or firm commitment to yourself in the following 6-paragraph manner, which I refer to as the *Self-confidence Formula*:

*I know that I have the ability to get a high-paying job that pays 'x' per month and 'y' per year, to take my lifestyle to an amazing new level.*

*I therefore demand of myself persistent, aggressive and continuous action towards getting it.*

*I realize that the dominating thoughts of my mind eventually reproduce themselves in outward, bodily action, and gradually transform themselves into physical reality.*

*Therefore I will concentrate my mind for thirty minutes daily upon the task of thinking of the highly-paid personality I want to become, by creating a mental picture of this personality and then transforming that picture into reality through practical service.*

*I fully realize that no wealth or position can long endure, unless built upon truth and justice, therefore I will engage in no transaction which does not benefit all whom it affects.*

*I will sign my name to this formula, commit it to memory and repeat it aloud twice a day with faith that it will gradually influence my entire life so that I will become a successful, highly-paid and happy worker in my chosen field of endeavor.*

*Signed:*_____

Decide on the amount of money you want to earn and make this entire 6-paragraph commitment in your notebook and sign.

Here's an example:

*I know that I have the ability to get a high-paying job that pays $8,000 per month and $96,000 per year, to take my lifestyle to an amazing new level...*

_____

_____

_____

_____

_____

_____

_____

_____

_____

_____

_____

_____

_____

*Signed:* <u>*Sly N*</u>

Read your commitment every morning when you wake up from sleep and every night before falling asleep. It will gradually increase your desire and change your self-esteem (or belief about yourself). And as such, it will enable you to feel comfortable to charge and go after far more than your current salary.

## 10. Habit # 10 – Self-discipline and Focus

One of the greatest challenges we have as humans is to give ourselves a command and respect it. This is a weakness that is common with far too many people.

Will you keep to your commitment of getting a high-paying job whatever it takes?

If you don't keep your focus on your job-getting goals and discipline yourself to consistently take action, you might not see any results.

## 11. Habit # 11 – Building A Personality Brand

You are a brand. That's how others look at you. Everything you do online and offline will be used to judge and rate you.

What do you want people, especially the hiring manager, to know about you? That's the message you should try to get across in your every action.

Your Facebook and LinkedIn profiles, your photos, etc - everything about you will either build your reputation as a reliable expert in your field or break it. So watch your personal brand.

## 12. Habit # 12 – Keeping Good Health

Health is everything. Without good health, you may not achieve your goals – especially getting the job you want.

Take time to eat healthy food. Exercise regularly to drive out stress and keep fresh blood and energy pumping into your system.

Get enough rest and sleep. Drink lots of water to purify your system. Your body is your temple of energy. Take good care of it!

If you follow most, or all of these 12 habits, you will completely transform your mind and personality to that of a winner.

And once your mind is conditioned to that of a winner, and ready for consistent action, you'd have earned your *insurance against failure*, as you'd have learned the art of turning failure (or temporary defeat) to opportunity.

Now, let's move on to the next Step…

# The Job getting Formula

## STEP 2

### Do You Know The Employer's PROBLEMS And DESIRES, Better Than Any Other Candidate? (Here's What They'll Pay You As High As Possible To Solve)

What a stunning discovery!

In 2009, over a thousand of the world's leading companies were asked, in a survey conducted by a group of experts, whether they have a problem of lack of skills within their workforce.

More than 750 (or 75%) of them said they have a *lack of skills* problem in their organization.

And over 500 (or 50%) said this same lack of skills was a big issue holding them back from growing their business.

So, why is this "skill gap" statistics… as experts call it… a BIG deal for you… when it comes to getting a high-paying job?

To answer this question, let's first of all understand the real meaning of a skill gap.

The dictionary defines a skill as *"the learned capacity to carry out pre-determined results, often with minimum time, energy, or both."*

We all know what the word gap means. It's like a "hole" or "space" in an object.

So, if an employee is said to have a "skill gap", it means that, there's one or more *key skills* that the employee is lacking to continue delivering the changing goals of an organization. In order words, the employee can no longer solve some emerging problems the company is facing.

At the level of an organization, career experts define a *skill gap* as *"a significant gap between an organization's current capabilities and the skills it needs in its employees to achieve its goals."*

It is the point at which an organization can no longer grow or remain competitive, because it cannot fill critical jobs with employees who have the right knowledge, skills, experience and abilities.

What causes the change in an organization's goals?

Simple! They have to look for new ways of doing things… in order to reach and satisfy more customers and make more profits for their shareholders.

They have to design new products and services, exploit new technology, sell more, reduce cost, etc.

For example, imagine a guy who was marketing manager for his former company or employer, then he moved to take up the position of Facebook Advertising Manager for another prestigious company that paid him twice his previous salary.

This is certainly because he mastered the *new* Facebook marketing skill which is newly *in demand* in the market. The company that hired him and doubled his salary did not have anybody within their company who mastered this new skill.

In other words, that company had a skill gap in Facebook marketing. You follow?

Now that we are clear about the term skill gap, let's get back to our question: *Why is this skill gap statistics a BIG deal for you?*

Simple answer: If a big number of companies are complaining of skill gaps among their workforce, it simply tells you that there is a

HUGE opportunity in high-paying jobs for you to exploit…especially if you just know how to.

But there's still another ONE IMPORTANT CONDITION: *You MUST have the required skills.* And I will show you easy ways to quickly develop such skills.

You see, while there happens to be huge unemployment, what many people don't know is about the "hidden" problem of *lack of skills* among organizations.

SKILL GAPS ARE THE GOLD MINES TO EXPLORE in order to find high-paying jobs.

So, how can we find and fill skill gaps to get high-paying jobs?

Answer: We find out which skills are in great demand and adapt ours accordingly.

From first sight, this strategy may seem complicated to follow. But in practice, it is the most *simple, appropriate* and *wisest* thing to do.

I'll show you the step-by-step *blueprint* on how to do that in a moment.

But for now, let's continue to nail down this very important skill gap thing further – because, if you don't get it right, ALL other things won't work.

You'll have to permit me to be a little harsh at this point, because… I don't care about the type of powerful résumé you have. All I know is that, if you get the "skills" part of the equation wrong, every other thing you do will *definitely* NOT WORK!

EVEN "20 YEARS EXPERIENCE" WON'T WORK!

Why? Because, the *"number of years of experience"* thing is a MYTH!

You're probably saying: "Sylvester, what the heck are you saying? Are you suggesting that experience doesn't really matter?"

Well… calm down and let me explain.

You see, most people wrongly think that employers are looking for a *number of years* of experience. In actual fact, employers are looking for the "skills gained" as a result of experience – not *necessarily* the number of years of experience. See the difference?

For example, let's take two job seekers who are applying for a job that requires BOTH *general marketing* skills and *Facebook advertising* skills.

Let's assume that the first guy has 5 years of *total marketing* experience which includes 3 months of *Facebook marketing* experience - acquired just *a couple of months* after Facebook was launched, in 2004.

Imagine this first guy competing with a second marketing guy from another company, who has 20 years of *total marketing* experience WITHOUT any *Facebook advertising* experience – and therefore NO Facebook advertising *skills*.

Which of them do you think would get the job of *Facebook advertising manager* for a prestigious company wanting to immediately start making money through Facebook advertising?

Again, note that the employer is looking for "Facebook marketing" skills. To them, that's like GOLD, because of the millions of dollars they plan to make through Facebook advertisements.

They want *results-achieving skills,* in this case, "<u>how to set up and follow up on ads on Facebook that bring in money</u>", and NOT a particular number of years of experience.

Who wins the job? Of course, the guy with 5 years experience, which includes 3 months of Facebook Advertising experience.

And here's the kicker:

It doesn't really matter how he acquired this skill. It may be that he voluntarily helped a friend who has a small business sell his products on Facebook, as a means of learning and applying this vital skill.

Whatever the means of acquisition, what is important is the skills and the way you demonstrate to the employer that you've mastered them.

And so, the *smart* first guy who was watching how the *skills market* for his industry is changing, did a wise thing to learn some Facebook advertising just a couple of months after Facebook came into existence in February 2004.

Brilliant, isn't that?

So, if you stop to think of it, SKILL IS THE REAL ASSET IN THE JOB WORLD. It is where the MONEY lies.

It is what employers are looking for – day in, day out!

Note that, although this example has to do with Facebook, the whole concept of *in-demand skills* and *skill gaps* is not only limited to Facebook or the Internet.

In fact, it is a general problem that arises when changes in economy take place, either due to technology or other change drivers.

This is how high-paying jobs are created in the business world, in any economy – good or bad.

After all, if it is bad for some people, it is certainly good for others. When somebody dies, a coffin seller makes a sale.

That does not mean that we pray for people to die. It's just a way to say employers create businesses that must solve real world problems in order to make money - and one of them is "how to package a corpse for burial through the use of a coffin." Get the point?

That justifies why employers are hunting for people with the right skills to solve those problems as they arise – same in a good as in a bad economy.

In a good economy, their problem is usually to sell more. In a bad economy, their problem is usually to cut down spending so as to maximize their profits as they sell less. So, you might just need to tweak your skills to be at their service through all times.

Now, what happens to the second marketing guy with his 20 years experience?

Well, I think he too has several options:

1. He may find out and learn from what made him lose a job opportunity to a young manager with a far fewer number of years of experience.

2. He might be close to retirement, in which case he might be getting some retirement benefits soon. That is, in a case where there are such benefits.

3. He may completely neglect the issue and classify it as *simple bad luck*. With this last option, let's see what happens if he works in an industry that is OBLIGED to use Facebook as a marketing "vehicle" – and therefore requires a continuous need of Facebook Advertising skills, going into the future:

   • Then, he may be doomed to "bad luck" forever.

   • In the worst case, he might be laid off, as his position becomes *redundant* – a term used by career professionals to describe a worthless job position in an organization's growth strategy.

   • Also, he may NEVER understand the depth of one of the biggest questions that drives every employer's hiring decision – the same question as the title of this Step of the Job-getting Formula, which is: *"Do you know the employer's PROBLEMS and DESIRES, better than any other candidate?"*

Like this second guy, and from my years of personal observation, that's how 990 out of every 1000 job seekers live their professional lives, without ever knowing how significant changes in the "skills market" are directly affecting their future.

The question at this point is:

# Will This Trend Of Skill Shortage Continue Into The Future?

To answer this question, let's look at the major causes of skills shortage.

It turns out that there are 2 major causes of skills shortage:

1. **Knowledge And Technology-driven Economy.** Technology and Knowledge are changing fast and so are the ways of doing business. And this rapid change of knowledge and technology will certainly continue in the future.

2. **Global Competition for Skilled Workers.** The world today is operated by a global economy with increasing competition driven by facilities in information and communication technology.

   Most companies focus on staying competitive, so they often outsource production to developing countries with the lowest labor costs (low-cost, acceptable and good-quality skills), and cheap standards of living.

   For example, it's a fact that job seekers in more developed countries such as in Canada, the United States, Europe and others cannot compete with those of equal qualifications and skills in low-wage countries such as in India, China, Africa, parts of the Middle East, and others, for a given type of job – e.g. I.T, manufacturing, and other online jobs.

   Such movements of jobs even in job sectors other than IT, e.g. manufacturing, will continue to operate as the global economic dynamic, with its accelerating pace and efficiency of technology continue to play forward.

As you can see, there will always be the combination of skills shortage, unemployment and demand for new skills going forward into the future.

So the next question is…

# How Can You Really Stay On Top Of All These? (How Can You WIN In The Mix Of Skills Shortage, Unemployment And Demand For New Skills?)

Here are 3 Key Strategies to WIN in this New Economy:

- **Key Strategy #1: Know your Strengths.** These changes in the global economy require YOU to think in new ways about what your biggest job opportunities are in the future.

  You also need to sharpen your ability to sell your skills to employers. The Job-getting Formula will help you enormously in this regard.

- **Key Strategy #2: Watch the Skills Market.** YOU need to keep an eye on the skills market and see where it is going and adapt your skills accordingly, in order to keep having a job or to get a new one. Know which skills are high in demand and which growing companies need those skills. Again, in this Step 2 of the Job-getting Formula, I will show you how.

But note this:

THERE'S NOTHING LIKE "JOB SECURITY" ANYMORE!

It doesn't exist or maybe it existed in the 1950s – in the industrial age. In this new global economy, driven by technology and opportunities for cheap labor, job security is simply an illusion. The phrase "job security" itself is an oxymoron (aka words that contradict each other). A job is only available if there is a problem to solve. If the problem can be solved by cheaper technology or cheaper labor, or ceases to be a problem due to some market forces, the person having the job ceases to have a job. In other words, a job by nature is insecure, for as long as it even exists. That's why those seeking job security (an oxymoron) are not different from morons.

- **Key Strategy #3**: **Always keep your skills up-to-date.** Your number of competitors, made up of the ruthless monster called "technology" and other people of the same skill set, for any given job, continues to rise *exponentially* at any given time.

But that same technology is putting *cutting-edge knowledge* and *skills* in the hands of ANYONE who has a computer and internet connection, regardless of their earthly location. So, you too can learn new skills as they come up.

Your professional and personal development should be your TOP priority, followed by your job-getting skills.

Here's great advice from Jim Rohn, America's Foremost Business Philosopher: *"Work harder on yourself than you do on your job."* He went on to say: *"Working at your job will earn you a living, but working on yourself (your skills) will earn you a fortune."*

Simply develop a passion for life-long, goal-oriented learning and personal development, in both formal and informal settings. I learned most of the highly-paid skills and personal success secrets, a hundred times more through informal means – in books, videos, webinars, online courses, seminars, etc., than I ever did in high-school, college or university.

When it comes to ways to develop and update your skills, the possibilities are endless. Consider certification, vocational training, JDs, PhDs & MBA programs, books, workshops, seminars, conferences, webinars, Youtube videos, online training or distance-learning, etc.

You don't need job security, because you surely won't get it, even if you wanted it so badly. You need a formula for constantly figuring out what problems employers have and the skills they are looking to pay highly for. That will keep you ahead of the game, from one high-paying job to another, while others around you struggle, see their incomes shrink, and live in fear and anxiety forever.

# How To Figure Out The EXACT Problem An Employer Is WILLING To Pay As Much As Possible To Hire You To Solve

Here's the powerful, field-tested, step-by-step, blueprint I have been using to unlock "hidden" high-paying job opportunities, both full-time and consulting, from companies.

If you apply this approach to your job search, you'd be far ahead of the competition and it will get you the high-paying job you want.

## Preliminary Research

1. Make a list of 10 companies you want to work for. Make sure the companies you choose belong to industries that are growing financially and are most likely to continue to grow over the next 20 years.

   If you choose a company that does not belong to a fast growing industry, you'd better change your choice immediately.

   A quick way to determine which industries are the fastest growing is to type in the words "Country Name +fastest growing industries (or companies)" or "Continent or Sub-region's Name +fastest growing industries (or companies)" into Google's search box and check out the search results you get.

   For example: "USA +fastest growing industries/companies", "China +fastest growing companies/industries", "Asia +fastest growing companies/industries", "Central Africa +fastest growing companies", "West Africa +fastest growing companies/industries", etc.

2. Refine your search while studying the fast-growing industries or companies by doing some research and finding answers to the following questions:

   a. What are the hot spots – where growth is concentrated either by a specific group of products or services or by specific geographic area?

   b. Which skills are in demand?

   c. How likely is the industry prone to outsourcing and off-shoring?

   d. And more.

3. Read local business journals, industry publications and professional or trade association newsletters to contemplate opportunities. Think like a private investigator while doing your research – be curious and questioning.

4. Search for the companies' annual reports, monthly/quarterly newsletters and letters to shareholders and read about how the companies did last year as well as their vision and goals for the current and future years.

5. Create a Google Alert about each company's name, so that anything that's published about the company online will automatically be sent to your email every time. This is a very simple but powerful research technique.

   a. Type in, or copy and paste www.google.com/alerts directly into your browser, or go to google.com and type in "Google Alerts" in the search box

   b. After the Google Alerts window opens, against the field labeled "Search query:", type in "[name of Company] [name of country/state]".

   c. Against field labeled "Deliver to:" type in your email address. Then click on the "Create Alert" button. And you're done. It's simple, but almost magical as you'll see when you start receiving info about your list of companies in your inbox.

6.  For each company in your Top-10 list, find out who runs the department in which you want to work.

    For large and medium size companies, they may be called Heads of Departments, Directors, Vice presidents of [name of department], Chief [name of department] Officers (e.g. Chief Marketing Officer), General Manager of [name of department] (like General Manager of Sales), etc.

    For very small companies, it might be the owner of the company themselves.

    You can find out who runs the department by looking at the firm's website or by simply calling the Company and asking who is responsible for that department. Or by searching, as follows, in Google: *Vice president of [name of department]* + *"[Name of Company]"* or *Director of [name of department]* + *"[Name of Company]"* or *General Manager of [name of department]* + *"[Name of Company]"* or any other appellation above.

7.  For each Company in your Top-10 list, create a networking relationship with 1 to 3 of their current employees, all of whom must be in the department you want to work for. This is for accurate information-getting, as we'll see later.

    **Note**: When choosing people for the purpose of networking and information-getting, choose people who are high up the hierarchy ladder. They are mostly the ones who have a great insight into the company's strategy and could give you more reliable information.

    If you don't physically know anybody working in the company, you can start creating your network in that company by finding out and going to the places where people of that company usually visit, such as trade shows, public events, seminars, conferences, restaurants, etc. Then meet them and interact with them.

Another easy way is to join LinkedIn.com and other social networking sites like Facebook.

Here are the steps to connect with current employees of the department you're interested in, using LinkedIn:

a.  Join LinkedIn.com

b.  Click on "Advance Search" next to the search box.

c.  Type in the search parameters. Fill the "country name" and "company name".

d.  Under Company, between "current or past", select "current" and click on the search button.

e.  Hover your mouse over the search results and find someone who can be a good match, from their working title, to act as your informant. Once selected, click on "Add to network". You'll be taken to the next stage.

f.  If you are prompted to enter an email address, do so if you have it.

    If you don't have their email, then there's another way out:

    If you have a dialogue that gives you options such as whether you are a "colleague", "classmate", "group member", "friend", "we've done business together", etc, then simply select *"We've done business together"* (assuming you've met them offline, like in a restaurant, but didn't get their email) and then, select the name of your current and past employers (since those are the only options you'd find). You may then type in a little introductory message. Then, click the "Send Invitation" button.

g.  After they respond to your invitation, ask them if they do work under the person running the department you are interested in. If they say no, ask them to refer you to somebody working in that department.

Once you find a person working in that department, try to connect with them on a deeper level. You can ask for their Facebook ID or find them on Facebook by their name and connect with them as well.

The idea is to increase your level of interaction with them.

Another way is to find something that may be of interest to them and give it to them. It may be something physical such as a "friendship" gift, or any other gadget or something intellectual you may find interesting, such as a free report, a video, an article online, etc. You can also suggest them to join a group on LinkedIn, Facebook, etc. Once they realize you care about their interests, they'll also care about yours.

And all this relationship-building stuff doesn't have to take you more than a month, a week or two, to complete. As a matter of fact, it can take a few days. You just need to be focused.

You may then even invite them for a drink or for lunch by telling them that you have a few questions to ask them about their company. Or you may simply keep your interactions with them strictly online. Ask for their email and phone number.

Whatever the case, ask them if they can offer you 10-15 minutes of their time for you to ask them a few questions about their company. Tell them that you can do it through phone or Skype, or both of you can agree to meet somewhere for lunch.

**Note**: If for any reason, someone is *particularly* not willing to answer your questions, move to the next person in your list of three current employees who work in the same department.

If however, they chose to answer your questions, DO NOT be satisfied with just the point of view of one "informant" alone. It's more effective to interview at least 2 or 3 people working for the same department in order to have a clear insight into the department's major problems – their biggest fears, frustrations, challenges and goals.

## The Gold-digging Questions

Once they accept your request for a few questions, get ready to call them on phone or Skype, or meet them physically and ask them *one or more* of the four sets of gold-digging questions below.

The aim of these questions is to dig deep into the "root" (I call it the "Gold") of the department's fears, frustrations, challenges and goals, which are most valuable to them – for which they will be willing to do anything or hire anyone to help resolve.

Get a pen and a pad ready to take detailed notes while they respond to your questions. This is ABSOLUTELY important.

Start by saying *"Hi [**Informant's Name**], I am doing some research about [**Name of industry in which the company belongs**] in order to stay informed of some of the real work challenges involved and your company is top of my list. And since you work there, may I ask you a few questions… that won't take more than 15minutes of your precious time… to help me gain clear insight?"*

Then, continue with one or more sets of the following gold-digging questions. Two sets of Gold-digging questions, e.g. "Biggest Challenge and Biggest Goal" or "Biggest Fear and Biggest Goal" or "Biggest Frustration and Biggest Goal", is usually optimal. You can also copy and paste or re-type the opening script above plus the gold-digging questions and send – through email or Facebook – for them to answer and return to you. But with this last option, you may have to follow up and maybe re-ask the questions on the phone and have them recite the answers for you to take notes – this way, it'll be easier for them as well.

## I. Gold-digging Questions based on Employer's Biggest Challenge

1. What is your Department's Biggest Challenge right now, with regards to Service and Best Practice?

   _____

   _____

   _____

2. What does the Head of your Department think is the solution to [this biggest challenge]? And why?

3. What other problems is [this biggest challenge] causing (or likely to cause)? And why?

   - Problem N#1:_____
   - Problem N#2:_____
   - Problem N#3:_____

4. What will happen if [Problem N#1] is not solved? And why?

   _____

   _____

   _____

5. What will happen if [Problem N#2] is not solved? And why?

   _____

   _____

   _____

6. What will happen if [Problem N#3] is not solved? And why?

_____

_____

_____

7. What if [this biggest challenge] *is overcome* such that all 3 problems you've just listed *are avoided*? How will that affect the Head of Department, team members, performance, reputation, image, or "life" of the Department?

_____

_____

_____

8. On a scale of 1 to 10, with 1 being not important at all, and 10 being extremely important, how important is it to the Department to overcome [this biggest challenge]? Please choose a number from 1 to 10.

___/**10**

## II. Gold-digging Questions based on Employer's Biggest Goal

1. What is your Department's Biggest Goal (or Objective) right now, with regards to Service and Best Practice?

_____

_____

_____

2. What does your Head of Department think is the solution to achieving [this biggest goal]? And Why?

_____

_____

_____


3.  What other goals must be achieved for this goal to be achieved? And Why?

    - Goal N#1:_____
    - Goal N#2:_____
    - Goal N#3:_____

4.  What will happen if [Goal N#1] is not achieved? And why?

    _____

    _____

    _____


5.  What will happen if [Goal N#2] is not achieved? And why?

    _____

    _____

    _____


6.  What will happen if [Goal N#3] is not achieved? And why?

    _____

    _____

    _____


7.  What if [this biggest goal] *is achieved* such that all the 3 goals you've listed *are achieved*? How will that affect the Head of Department, team members, performance, reputation, image, or "life" of the Department?

    _____

    _____

    _____

8.  On a scale of 1 to 10, with 1 being not important at all, and 10 being extremely important, how important is it to the Department to achieve [this biggest goal]? Please choose a number from 1 to 10.

    ___ /10

### III. Gold-digging Questions based on Employer's Biggest Fear

1.  What's the Biggest Fear in your department right now, with regards to Service and Best Practice?

    _____

    _____

    _____

2.  What does the Head of your Department think is the solution to [this biggest fear]? And why?

3.  What other problems is [this biggest fear] causing (or likely to cause)? And why?

    - Problem N#1:_____
    - Problem N#2:_____
    - Problem N#3:_____

4.  What will happen if [Problem N#1] is not solved? And why?

    _____

    _____

    _____

5.  What will happen if [Problem N#2] is not solved? And why?

_____

_____

_____

6.  What will happen if [Problem N#3] is not solved? And why?

    _____

    _____

    _____

7.  What if [this biggest fear] *is managed* such that all 3 problems you've just listed *are avoided*? How will that affect the Head of Department, team members, performance, reputation, image, or "life" of the Department?

    _____

    _____

    _____

8.  On a scale of 1 to 10, with 1 being not important at all, and 10 being extremely important, how important is it to the Department to manage [this biggest fear]? Please choose a number from 1 to 10.

    ___/<u>10</u>

### IV. Gold-digging Questions based on Employer's Biggest Frustration

1.  What is your Department's Biggest Frustration right now, with regards to Service and Best Practice?

_____

_____

_____

2. What does the Head of your Department think is the solution to [this biggest frustration]? And why?

3. What other problems is [this biggest frustration] causing (or likely to cause)? And why?

   - Problem N#1:_____
   - Problem N#2:_____
   - Problem N#3:_____

4. What will happen if [Problem N#1] is not solved? And why?

_____

_____

_____

5. What will happen if [Problem N#2] is not solved? And why?

_____

_____

_____

6. What will happen if [Problem N#3] is not solved? And why?

_____

_____

_____

7. What if [this biggest frustration] *is solved* such that all 3 problems you've just listed *are avoided*? How will that affect the Head of Department, team members, performance, reputation, image, or "life" of the Department?

_____

_____

_____

8. On a scale of 1 to 10, with 1 being not important at all, and 10 being extremely important, how important is it to the Department to overcome [this biggest frustration]? Please choose a number from 1 to 10.

____/10

## Situational Assessment Questions

From the answers you'll get after asking the gold-digging questions, you may need to properly assess the current situation based on information about the Head of Department, the department, and the company at large. You may then need to ask *one* or *many* of the following situational assessment questions. They are listed here from 'a' to 'z'. Equally take detailed notes as you ask:

a. For how long have you been working with [name of person running the department], and how is your working relationship?

b. What kind of person is [Name of person running department]?

c. What kind of manager is he/she?

d. What does [Name of person running department] look for in an employee?

e. How is [Name of person running department] positioned in the Company?

f. How is [Name of person running department] generally considered by the rest of the Company regarding his personality or personal style?

g. Is [Name of person running department] little or highly respected by the president, general manager or owner of the company?

h. Are there any rumors or possibilities of [Name of person running department] moving up the hierarchy any time from now, or will he/she become more stable in his present role?

i. Where does he source for his/her people?

j. What type of people does he/she hire?

k. What was his/her most recent or biggest achievement?

l. Is the department meeting its expectations and growing?

m. Is the department under pressure for not meeting its expectations?

n. What type of culture is reigning in the department?

o. Is the department more or less respected by the company?

p. How is the department doing compared to other departments in the company?

q. What's the biggest thing the department needs to do to meet or exceed their expectations?

r. What new products or services is the company looking to create or offer in the near future?

s. How is the company doing financially and what can you say about its future growth?

t. Which companies are the company's biggest competitors?

u. What "one thing" does the company need to do in order to beat the competition?

v.   Who are the company's best customers?

w.   Who would they like to have as customers?

x.   What do customers think of the company?

y.   What position does the company hold in the marketplace? Is it a recognized leader or simply lost in the ocean of competitors?

z.   What can you say about the company regarding its vision, its policies, its people and its culture?

## About The "Gold Digger's Approach" Of "Finding-The-Problem-And-Solving-It" – Why It Works Best And Easiest To Get You A *High-paying* Job

The job search strategy that is well known and understood by many… is that of waiting for jobs to be published on job boards before applying.

The problem with this strategy, especially in an era where the number of jobseekers competing for jobs is high, is that:

The job opening may be known long before it is announced by the jobseekers or contenders who initiated its creation in the first place. They might have known by priory and directly contacting the hiring manager or head of department and expressing their abilities and willingness to help the company solve its pressing problems.

When this happens, and the job vacancy is finally published, it becomes very difficult to compete with someone who has been following through from the very beginning.

Proactive job seekers, those I call the active **job-getters**, spend their time studying a certain company or a group of companies as it evolves over time and prepare themselves by learning new skills and developing their strengths in the direction of the companies' needs.

Also, most often, when employers have a pressing need to fill, they often go looking for the best candidate themselves, without passing through recruiting firms or doing open postings.

They prefer to deal with a handful of good-to-great candidates that, they think, can solve their problems. And they usually find them through referrals from friends, colleagues and other close connections, as well as through rapid searches on sites like LinkedIn and Google.

So, if you are counting on the openly advertised positions, then your chances of picking a high-paying job fast may be very slim. It may take you years, instead of months, to find a good job, if you continue to play by the old rules.

Also, with the old, most popular job hunting approach, people apply for numerous positions, often with generic résumés, and expect the employer to read through their résumés to figure out how they can be useful to the employer. This is a grossly ineffective approach.

Now, you might be asking:

What could be wrong with increasing my chances by applying for as many open job positions as I possibly can, with a generic, 3 to 5-page résumé, which is packed-full of work experience and other necessary details?

This is a fair question – especially considering how unique, highly-targeted and "out-of-the-ordinary" my recommended "find-the-problem-and-solve-it" approach may sound.

But, here's a "thought-provoking" example for you:

Let's say that you have neck pain, and you decide to go see the doctor to prescribe you some medicine to make the pain go away.

You meet the doctor and tell him of your pain.

The question is:

WHAT WILL THE DOCTOR DO, AND WHY?

Well, if he's like most great doctors he will, after proper diagnosis, prescribe you one of the many drugs that cure neck pain, e.g. Tylenol.

Now, stop for a minute and imagine that you're sitting there across from the doctor and, instead of prescribing you a drug, he hands you a *thick medical journal* to read through and figure out, for yourself, what could *possibly* be the treatment for your neck pain...

...And he doesn't even care about the fact that you won't be able to read through even a couple of pages, because of your neck pain – needless to mention reading the whole journal.

Question: Would you listen to such a doctor? Would you even pick up the medical journal to read it?

Of course not.

But why?

Why would someone not *logically* want a medical journal that "has the cure for everything?"

Well, it turns out that, we humans aren't often "logical" – especially when we are sick or driven by the pain of a serious problem.

When we have a painful problem or burning desire, we want ONLY things that sound like they're made to fix our specific problem or satisfy our particular desire. And we avoid things that sound like "they have the cure for everything."

Hiring managers and hiring decision makers are just like any other human being, with their own share of desires and big problems.

And to make things worse, they are very busy people, who live in an over-communicated world.

So, only résumés and cover letters that speak to their greatest and specific problems (or desires) will grab their attention.

They want you to show them that you've already figured out what they want, and that you are passionate, willing, and able to help.

And that's *exactly* what this unique, Gold Digger's approach of "finding-the-problem-and-solving-it" aims at.

The gold-digger's approach of problem-finding is made up of a combination of one or more of the 4 sets of gold-digging questions and *a few* or *many* of the situational assessment questions, as we just saw in the previous section.

Once you've figured out the real problem of the employer, by asking them those questions, you'd have found "GOLD." You'd have figured out what the employer really wants – what they are willing to do *anything* or pay any price to solve. You'd have successfully mastered more than eighty percent of the way that leads to a high-paying job (the type of job that will make you big money to pay part of your debts and take your life to a whole new level).

Here's an example of how to apply the gold-digging questions in your job search:

Let's assume you want to work as Legal Advisor/Consultant in the Legal Department of a telecommunications company (which belongs to a fast growing industry). Assuming you are talking to one of the people working in that department, here's how you'll apply the set of gold-digging questions that deals with the Biggest Fear.

YOU: *"Hi, I am doing some research about [the Telecommunications Industry], in order to stay informed of some of the real work challenges involved and your company is top of my list. And since you work there, may I ask you a few questions… that won't take more than 15minutes of your precious time… to help me gain clear insight?"*

INFORMANT: *"Sure. Go ahead… hope it'll be brief."*

YOU: question1 *"What's the Biggest Fear in your department right now, with regards to Service and Best Practice?"*

INFORMANT: *"Well… our biggest issue right now is to avoid poorly written contracts."*

YOU: ^question2 *"What does your head of department think is the solution to [this issue of poorly written contracts]? And Why?"*

INFORMANT: *"He thinks the solution to this problem is to get managers of every department, especially sales managers, to get their customer contracts reviewed by the legal department before being approved into execution."*

YOU: ^question3 *"What other problems is [this issue of poorly written contracts] causing (or likely to cause)? And why?"*

INFORMANT: *"It is causing us 'problems in our relationships with customers' and 'potential lawsuits'."*

YOU: ^question4 *"What will happen if you have [relationship problems with customers]? And why?"*

INFORMANT: *"We might lose some of our customers."*

YOU: ^question5 *"What will happen if you end up in [lawsuits with customers]? And why?"*

INFORMANT: *"That might lead us to paying out financial indemnities to customers, making us lose money."*

YOU: ^question7 *"What if [this issue of poorly written contracts] is managed such that all the problems you've just mentioned (i.e. [relationship problems with customers] and [lawsuits with customers] ) are avoided? How will that affect the head of department, team members, performance, reputation, image and 'life' of the department?"*

INFORMANT: *"Well... the head of department and everybody in the department will be happy and we'll be highly recognized and respected by the Managing Director."*

YOU: ^question8 *"On a scale of 1 to 10, with 1 being not important at all, and 10 being extremely important, how important is it to the department to solve [this problem of poorly written contracts]? Please choose a number from 1 to 10."*

INFORMANT: *"9/10"*

Now, think about this example for a minute. Do you see how extremely effective these gold digging questions are?

If followed and applied correctly, they have the ability to dig deep and bring out the REAL problems the department is facing, and for which they are willing to do anything to find a solution.

The beauty of this gold digger's approach is that it helps you get far beyond the "superficial problems" the department is facing and go deep into their *high-impact* and *high-value* implications for the Company's business success.

These are the types of problems the hiring manager or head of department is focused on solving, especially given the fact that it is 9 out of 10 on the scale of importance. These are the types of problems that, if addressed in your résumé and cover letter, will make all the difference and separate you from the thousands of ordinary applicants or job seekers out there. These are the types of problems the hiring manager or head of department is expecting to "see" in a résumé or cover letter. Only suggestions and proposals about solving these types of problems can get their attention.

For example, let's consider these two Objective Summaries from the résumés of two different candidates seeking to get the same job of Legal Advisor/Consultant, from the same telecommunications company, as in our previous example.

The first says:

***Objective Summary1:***

*Experienced Legal Advisor, seeking a challenging position in a fast growing telecommunications company where my 10 years of legal experience coupled with my analytical and legal skills can contribute to the success of the company.*

The second says:

### *Objective Summary2:*

*Help you STOP the problem of poorly-written contracts, caused by stubborn sales managers, in a way that will preserve good relationships with customers, secure the company from lawsuits and legal risks (like losing money through financial indemnities paid to customers), and enable you to gain the recognition of the Managing Director.*

Obviously, you guess the question I'm about to ask. There you go… if you were the Head of the Legal Department looking for a solution to your problem of poorly-written contracts, which of the two résumés will grab your attention? The second one, you bet. It touches on all that is important to the head of department or hiring manager in a very specific way. It shows that, without any guess work, the owner of the second résumé knows what he/she is talking about.

You can clearly notice that the first résumé's objective summary sounds like what every Jack will write. It's very generic. There's no sign or trust that the person having that résumé knows the real problems of the hiring manager or head of department. It's just blah, blah, blah. Another problem is that it is highly focused on the owner of the résumé rather than on *"what's in it for the hiring manager or head of department."* And worse still, it speaks to no particular individual, whereas, the second speaks to a person – take note of phrases like *"Help you…"* and *"…enable you gain the recognition of…"*

# Why (And How) Employers Pay Highly For Jobs That Solve Their Biggest Fears, Frustrations, Challenges And Goals

Want to know why and how employers pay highly for certain jobs?

The answer lies in how humans value things.

There are 3 major levels at which people value things: 1. *Physical* 2. *Emotional.* 3. *Intellectual.*

And the reason is that we have three brains that form one.

We have the physical brain, the emotional brain, and the intellectual brain.

Let's look at how we value things at the physical level. The physical brain is concerned with survival, security, and "making it out here in the real world." It likes to achieve success in the form of getting the things that it wants, like food, shelter and other physical things, such as property. It likes to avoid death, pain and physical loss of any sort. It will readily move away from these last three things.

In fact, a person will pay a lot more money to avoid death, pain and physical loss than to have more life, pleasure, and physical gains.

If you've ever had a serious tooth ache, stomach ache, back pain, or have been faced with a threat such as the bank or creditors threatening to seize some of your valuables like your car or house or anything important... or you've been engaged in a personal project that, if it fails, will lead to loss of property and family and friends laughing at you, then you know what I am talking about.

The second level at which we value things is emotional. The emotional brain is concerned with our feelings. It likes to move towards positive emotions like joy, happiness and love. And it will *readily* move

71

away from fear, anxiety, and all the things that don't feel good emotionally.

People will generally pay much more money to move away from fear, anxiety, and other disturbing and uncomfortable emotions than they'll pay for joy, love and happiness.

Note that the emotional brain is closely linked to the physical. And when we are faced with an eminent physical loss, death, or pain, it's our emotions that are firing and driving our decisions and actions.

(Note: It just makes it easier and simpler to understand to look at the physical and emotional brains separately. But in reality, they are closely linked.)

When we have experienced a physical pain or loss before, we fear to experience such a pain or loss in the future. The fear is the emotion. Even if we haven't physically experienced a pain or loss yet, the thought or visualization of it in our minds triggers the powerful emotions of fear and anxiety.

The third level at which we value things is intellectual. The intellectual brain moves towards understanding – feeling like we "get" what's going on. It wants to be right about things. It wants to have a predictable model that predicts what's going to happen. It also likes social status, power and control.

It will move away from confusion, frustration, worry, being out of control, and being wrong. It doesn't like when it thinks it gets something right and its model is proven wrong.

People will equally and *easily* spend more money to get someone to figure out things they don't know – to solve a pressing problem and avoid confusion, frustration, worry, and being out of control – than they will do to discover fresh knowledge that has no *immediate* problems to solve, or that has the tendency to prevent problems from occurring.

For example, in the case where you give a hiring manager your 5-page résumé to see the vast field of knowledge and experience you have and for them to figure out how you can be of help to them – this is not as important to them as solving their immediate problems.

That's why Eben Pagan, one of my marketing coaches, who is also one of the leading information marketing experts in the world, once said: *"People don't buy prevention, they buy solutions."* And mostly, they buy immediate solutions.

Psychologists have found that, we are twice more motivated by pain, fear, confusion, frustration and other *moving-away-from* motivators, than we are by pleasure, desire and other *moving-towards* motivators.

But, for both types of motivators:

1. The stronger the *moving-away-from* motivators (pain, loss, damage, fear, anxiety, discomfort, frustration, confusion, challenge, out of control, being wrong, no predictable model, etc.), the higher the value of the solution and the more people are *willing* to pay.

2. The stronger the *moving-towards* motivators (desire, pleasure, joy, happiness, financial gains, material gains, social status, recognition, predictable and secure solution, etc.), the higher the value of the solution, and the more people are *willing* to pay to get it.

As you can see, we act most of the time based on these "irrational motivators." Although we often exist under the illusion that we're making decisions and taking actions consciously, in reality, we are mostly driven by our irrational motivators. And we use our intellect to rationalize the impulse-driven decisions we've already made.

So what's my point with all this?

Simple:

The direct and simplest way to get a high-paying job is to look for the *"moving-away-from"* and *"moving-towards"* motivators of your prospective hiring manager or head of department and offer to help solve them.

That is why we use the gold-digging questions to find out, specifically, their biggest fear, biggest frustration, biggest challenge or biggest goal. Like in our previous example, take note of these irrational motivators. They have been underlined for clarity:

*Help you STOP the problem of poorly-written contracts caused by stubborn sales managers in a way that will <u>preserve good relationships with customers</u>, <u>secure the company from legal risks and lawsuits</u> (like <u>losing money through financial indemnities paid to customers</u>), and enable you to <u>gain the recognition of the Managing Director</u>.*

These are the things that motivate a hiring manager or hiring decision maker to take action and hire somebody immediately. This process happens even faster when there is urgency of results involved.

So if you are already in the picture, by being the first to contact the hiring manager, and if you followed the Gold digger's approach, you stand a better chance, favored by urgency of the situation, to be hired to solve the problem.

The interesting thing is that, people hardly take preventive action while a problem is still manageable. They often wait for it to get acute. That's why the gold digging questions are focused on the problems of the moment. All the first questions contain the words *"right now."* For example, *"What's the Biggest Fear in your department right now, with regards to Service and Best Practice?"*

Remember, "People don't buy prevention. People buy immediate solutions." But fortunately, there are always pressing problems to solve in a big or fast-growing company. And that's the type of company or business you want to work for. (And even those that are struggling to grow still have problems that can possibly offer great opportunities for well-paying jobs.)

So, if you can find a "pressing pain" a hiring manager or head of department is facing in their company and skillfully offer to help, then you have found "gold." You have an opportunity to get a high-paying job created for you from scratch – the kind of job that will help you pay your debts and offer you the lifestyle you really want.

If we consider our previous example, let's say the company has previously lost $1,000,000 dollars in the form of indemnities (liabilities or damages) paid to one customer after a lawsuit. And after that, the Managing Director is so "angry" that he instructed the Head of the Legal Department to *do everything he and his team can* to stop such a loss from happening again. The Head of the Legal Department is probably taking this problem very seriously because he knows if he and his team do not take action to stop these lawsuits from happening, then a future loss can lead to him being fired. That is the type of fear, pain and urgency I am talking about.

And if the head of department has such an emotional fear (of being fired) and the physical loss and pain (of having caused a great financial loss to the company in the past) coupled with the intellectual frustration that stubborn sales managers do not seem to be in compliance, and that they cannot figure out a clear solution to the problem, then he will (with approval from management) be *willing* to pay you even 10% of that *past* loss to help stop any further loss.

And if you do the math, 10% of $1,000,000 is a whopping $100,000 of annual salary or a little over $8,000 per month. And their "rationale" will be that they are making a very good financial decision – which is quite true – but which, in reality, was driven by their deep-seated emotional and irrational motivators. Bear in mind that, although this is just an example, it nonetheless helps to illustrate the point of how high-paying jobs are created from employers' biggest fears, challenges, frustrations and goals.

I know you might be saying that this is a form of prevention. Yeah, but not the type I am talking about. The type I am referring to – which is the type people *don't* buy very often – is preventing a problem that has *never* occurred in the past.

What we are dealing with here is really about *stopping* an *ongoing problem* from re-occurring. It is different from preventing a problem which has never happened from ever happening – without ever experiencing the pain of it in the past. Hope you get the idea?

I will teach you the skills of how to communicate the fact that you can help provide a solution to a hiring manager or hiring decision maker in the next Step of the Job-getting Formula… because in many cases, you really can help. All you need to do is ask other people, do a little research, read books, take some courses and do everything possible to find the answers.

For now, all we want to know is the result that they want, so that we can appeal to their needs later.

## How To Make Sure Your Competence Is Not Sabotaging Your Success

99 percent of people don't know of this new approach of find-the-problem-and-solve-it. They talk about their PhDs, MBAs, JDs, certifications and their many years of experience. None of these things are important to a hiring manager or hiring decision maker, if you don't show them how it is clearly related to solving their problems.

And for you to find out what their problems are, it's NOT enough to sit and imagine what problems your prospective employer is facing and come out with an answer or proposal.

You MUST ASK. You must dig far underneath the surface to get to the bottom of their highly-motivating needs. You must use the gold digging questions.

If we can get that right – if we can find that thing where all the value resides, then take all of the knowledge and experiences from our entire life and apply them to the problem, that's when we become a "product" that literally sells itself for a very high price or salary.

And the interesting thing is that, when this happens, it doesn't require a lot of selling, because if they even knew a solution existed they would want to pay for it immediately. They would want to hire you to solve their problems for a high salary and interesting benefits.

It doesn't hurt to do powerful, "below-the-radar" marketing on top of that, as we'll see in the next Step. It only helps.

But, what most people *wrongly* do is this:

They say *"here's my résumé. There's more than you need inside. Take it and figure out what you want and call me and I will be glad to help."*

And guess what? Nothing happens!

Why? Because, this is simply the WRONG way. It doesn't work that way anymore - especially in the present competitive job market.

You can struggle with the traditional method to get a job that pays *slightly* higher. But if you really want a high-paying job, that pays twice or three times your salary, you need to change your approach. Follow the Gold Digger's approach.

The right and better thing to do is to ask the gold-digging questions and come up with a list of 3 to 5 most important things your prospective hiring manager and decision maker wants and then take all your knowledge, experience, research, and all your creativity and street-smarts (another name for what you learn from your day-to-day, real life experiences), and focus them on getting your prospective hiring manager those results.

You simply ask yourself: *"What's everything I have learned in my whole life and how can I apply it to solve my prospective hiring manager's problem?"*

Even if the hiring manager (or employer) decides to publish the job position after you've contacted them and found out what they wanted, you'll still win. Most often they won't do that, if they have an urgent need.

But if they do, look at it this way:

You'll be competing with people who are less ready and unprepared at all levels – psychologically and physically. They just recently heard of the vacancy and have probably taken one night to make up what they think is a powerful résumé.

But you, on the contrary... have previously demonstrated (as I will continue to show you) to the hiring manger that *you know their problem better than any other candidate...* that you know what you're talking about – that you're the expert.

Most people dead-wrongly assume that... the fact that they have some experience coupled with a business degree, an MBA, a certification, a PhD, or any other specialized knowledge, and that, since there are many companies having business problems, they'll have many companies to help. And so, they sleep at night and dream of a wonderful tomorrow where everyone would be announcing positions and asking to be helped with their business problems. But the next day they wake up, and it's not the case. Reality kicks in again.

Being knowledgeable and experienced is just the ticket that gets you into the game. It's not the game itself.

The real game is to contact, influence and attract hiring managers and hiring decision makers. It's to convince them that you've got the goods, and then offer them so much value in the form of free knowledge (as I will show you in the next Step) that helps explain their problems to them better, in a way that builds trust and credibility. I will show you how to skillfully do that in the next Step.

Being knowledgeable and experienced, on the one hand, and knowing how to influence hiring managers and hiring decision makers to offer you a high-paying job, on the other, are two COMPLETELY separate domains of expertise.

It's so easy for us to stay with our ego and expertise and consider hiring managers as being stupid or as simply not understanding, that we are the ones that get it right, that they don't understand our value. It's so easy!

But at the same time, that's mostly the source of our problem of not being able to sell ourselves at success-sized salaries.

As Mark Twain said: *"It's not what you know that's the problem, it's what you know that isn't so, is the problem."*

Our own expertise is often the obstacle to selling and marketing ourselves.

So, you might be asking:

*"It seems like my expertise isn't adding a lot of value, following the traditional approach. So, should I just abandon my expertise? How much does the expertise really matter in the whole equation, if right now it's getting in the way?"*

My answer:

In the big scheme, your expertise doesn't really matter much. All that matters is that your prospect FEELS like you understand their problem. What matters is if they feel like they'll get what they want, if they hire you. Only after they hire you is your expertise useful. That's when you can show them what you know, in practice.

In the next Step, I will show you how to communicate your skills, experience, accomplishments, and other qualities of yours to the hiring manager, head of department or hiring decision maker in a way that builds a strong relationship, which facilitates and "pushes" them to call you for an interview.

Now that you've answered the second BIG QUESTION of the Employer (and of the Job-getting Formula), the next Step is to answer the third BIG QUESTION, which is...

# The Job getting Formula

## STEP 3

### Can You DELIVER RESULTS, Despite On-The-Job Challenges, Better Than Any Other Candidate? (Here's How To "Force" Them To Call You For An Interview)

OK. Now that you've successfully identified what the hiring manager, head of department or hiring decision maker wants, the next thing is to figure out how to respond to their needs...in a way that would make them offer you the opportunity to help – in other words, call you for an interview and eventually create a high-paying job for you.

In order to do that, you'll need to know how to move them to action, by using words to appeal to their emotions.

It's time to finally teach you some highly-kept secrets regarding influence.

First let me share with you four characteristics that all humans have in common. These four will help you understand how to shape your communication to make the hiring manager take action and call you for an interview.

(Now, consider me a "chimp", if you get a little too pissed off with what I'm about to say.)

Closely similar to higher animals such as *apes* (chimps for example), we share the following in common:

1. We have very poor impulse control, especially when it comes to things related to sex, status and survival.

2. We are "instant gratification" lovers. We're not very good at thinking about the future. We are much more motivated by instant, immediate results.

3. We are highly emotional – when we get happy, we want to give everyone a hug. When we get angry everyone becomes our enemy. (Yeah, I know you'll say you don't do that "animal stuff." But just take some time to observe.)

4. We're highly intelligent. But a gazillion times, we use our marvelous intelligence to the service of our "lower" physical, irrational and emotional needs, like sex, status and survival.

I hope you're not asking me… "How can you compare humans to animals like chimps and monkeys?"

Well, part of being human is being ANIMAL – is being "Senior Chimp."

I know we exist under the illusion that we're awake… that we're alert, that we're rational, that we're conscious decision makers, etc.

But the reality is… we're not always.

Remember I said we have a physical brain that is "linked" to our physical needs. And that we also have an emotional brain that takes care of our feelings or emotions. And a third intellectual or logical, thinking brain that does our thinking, reasoning and analysis.

But it has been found that these three brains are hardly synchronized with each other. The emotional and the physical brains always tend to *influence* the thinking of the intellectual brain.

There is a constant voice going on in our heads – "Do it, don't do it," "I can do it, you can't do it," "It's the right time, it's not the right time," etc. Most often, the emotional and physical brains win "influence" over the intellectual.

Consider for example, when we decide to get on a diet and tell ourselves that we won't eat a particular type of food or that we won't eat more than a certain quantity of food in a day, especially when we're no longer hungry, for whatever reason.

What usually happens when we come across food that looks really delicious – like our longtime favorite? And let's say we haven't eaten it for a long time. What happens?

Well, I guess saliva will rush down our throat before we even realize it has done so. Our emotions will immediately give a signal to our hands to try a pinch of it. We'll be "seeing" ourselves in our mind enjoying the food, and before we realize, we're already devouring it physically.

Then suddenly, we'd stop and ask, "What am I doing, for God's sake?" Too late, my friend. The deal is done.

But what do we tell ourselves after that?

We'd probably say… *"Hmmm… I think this is just for today. It will NEVER happen again"* or *"I just got a pinch of it, not too bad"* or *"Yeah, I was feeling a little bit hungry."* And the list goes on. You know… the possibilities of lying to ourselves are endless. We use our awesome intellect to rationalize our emotion-driven actions.

As I said before, we humans have an infinite capacity for self-deception. And it seems as if we are craftily-wired to mostly use our marvelous intelligence to satisfy our basic emotional, physical and irrational needs such as sex, survival and status. All other needs, such as relationships, money, etc., are influenced by these three basic needs.

So, how does all of these relate to having a high-paying job?

Answer: If you want to influence any hiring manager to offer you a high-paying job, you must know what their deepest physical, emotional and irrational needs are, and how these needs are linked to their "rational" or logical, superficial needs.

Remember at the end of Step 2, we said:

1. The stronger the *moving-away-from* motivators (pain, loss, damage, fear, anxiety, discomfort, frustration, confusion, challenge, out of control, being wrong, no predictable model, etc.), the higher the value of the solution and the more people are *willing* to pay for it.

2. The stronger the *moving-towards* motivators (desire, pleasure, joy, happiness, financial gains, material gains, social status, recognition, predictable and secure solution, etc.), the higher the value of the solution, and the more people are *willing* to pay to get it.

If a hiring manager has an objective to deliver a specific result (the superficial need) or else he/she gets fired, there is an underlying emotional need that has to be met. And that emotional need is the "fear of being fired" (or the drive to survive).

Likewise if a hiring manager must deliver a specific result in order to gain recognition or a promotion (or improved professional status – which is still linked to survival and sex)… the superficial and rational need is the specific result they want to achieve. So they may say: *"Our objective is that we must stop losing 50% of our sales to our competitors…"*

But here's the tricky part:

If you are talking about the specific result or superficial and rational need (like 99% of job seekers do, including those following advice from many of the so-called "job hunting experts" out there), and never addressing the underlying emotional and irrational needs – in this case, the "fear of being fired" or the "desire of being recognized," you *may* HARDLY move them to action.

If they are fired, they know they might lose their social status. Inside of them, there are other irrational fears going on. They know losing their job and social status might make it difficult for them to survive and have more sex. Again, it is these underlying needs that motivate them to take action and do everything to maintain their position. One of those actions could mean hiring you.

We all have these underlying "emotional hot buttons" or "irrational motivators" linked to our superficial needs. And those hot buttons can be triggered by laser-sharp and compelling communication...

...The type of communication that would move hiring managers, heads of departments and decision makers to the action you want... which is, calling you for an interview and offering you a high-paying job.

That's what I am about to teach you.

## The Wickedly-Effective 3 Mistakes Marketing™ Technique (3MM)

It is true that one killer weapon can make all the difference between successfully influencing a hiring manager to interview you or not. One of such weapons is my sneakily-simple, high-octane 3 Mistakes Marketing. I call it the 3MM, for short.

This is one of the most powerful interview-getting weapons I have used time and time again, to influence hiring managers and decision makers to offer me big-money jobs – both temporary consulting and permanent contract jobs.

This 3MM approach can "brutally-seduce" a hiring manager to create a job for you where there was supposed to be none. You just need to know how to use it. And I have made it stunningly simple and easy-to-implement for you. Try it, and you'll get almost unbelievable results.

As a learning example, I'll take you through one of my personal 3MM documents. I used it on one CEO of a fast-growing road transportation company and landed a lucrative contract job that consisted in hiring and supervising a fleet and a client account manager, establishing a Trucks Maintenance contract, and implementing a Maintenance and Transportation Management software solution.

(For privacy reasons, I have replaced the names of individuals and of the company with fictitious ones.)

You can download the documents by following these steps:

1. Logon to http://jobgettingformula.com/members/signup.php by entering your first name, last name, email and password. Make sure the "Terms and Conditions" box is checked.

2. Click on "Submit."

3. Once you're logged in, click on "My Tools And Samples."

4. Click on and download "3MM–PotterExpressCo.pdf."

Also download the following document (this was used to draft the 3MM):

"FearsFrustrationsGoalsChallenges-PotterExpressCo"

Read them entirely and let me show you how to put yours together.

Hope you've found your top-10 list of companies and have started doing some gold-digging research on them – because, without knowing what the hiring manager or hiring decision maker really wants, this 3MM technique won't work for you. It will be like throwing water on a duck's back.

You may get this same feeling of neutrality when you read my 3MM, because you're not having the same problems as the person it was addressed to. But if you direct yours to a specific hiring manager, with full and accurate knowledge of what they really want (or want to avoid), you'll create a magical response that will lead to a call for a job interview!

If you have a little luxury of time, I'd advise you to use 1 or 2 of the least important companies in your top-10 list as "guinea pigs" to experiment and gain master's level savvy with the concepts and techniques I am about to show you, before moving to your top-of-the-list favorite employers.

While I was struggling to come out with a job-getting formula for myself and others, I came across the book *"Influence: The Psychology of Persuasion,"* by Robert B. Cialdini, PhD. And in this book, Robert Cialdini talks about the 6 major weapons of influence.

In the coming sections of this Step of the Job-getting Formula, I will be discussing how I have *creatively* applied these weapons in my 3MM to get high-paying jobs and how you too can apply them to get the same results.

We'll discover the 6 weapons as we go along. You'll see how they have been skillfully woven into the 3MM, with other little-known weapons that I learned from other multi-million-dollar information marketing teachers, to make it wickedly-effective. It is a sneaky and below-the-radar approach to marketing yourself and your value.

In the next series of paragraphs, I will teach you how to use the 3MM technique to share useful information, build rapport, trust and credibility with any prospective hiring manager you want… in a way that would *literally* "push" them to call you for an interview and *probably* hire you!

I will be showing you "the ropes and the traps" of this technique… and how the 3MM "secret source" was all put together, within the framework of some step-by-step rules to follow.

## RULE OF INFLUENCE #0: Be Honest

Since we'll be studying some "bad-ass" weapons of influence that can really manipulate people, you'll need to bring your highest conscientious self to the game.

It is my sincere wish that you don't fall into the trap of self-deception – as this can cause you to be crazily dishonest with your offer – like promising things you cannot do.

So, at this stage, I want you to make an ethical and responsible commitment to yourself, such as: *"I'll do everything possible to deliver only quality service that meets the expectations of my prospective hiring manger."*

Please make the commitment here and sign:

_____

_____

Your Name and Signature here:_____

## RULE OF INFLUENCE #1: Think From The Perspective Of Your Prospective Hiring Manager

Hiring managers, just like other people, want a solution to their problems that sounds like it was proposed by someone who thinks like them.

Now, get this:

One of the things that differentiates us from lower animals is that we can do consequential or cause-and-effect thinking.

But here is where it gets interesting:

When we are faced with a pressing problem that causes emotional and physical pain, we lose our consequential thinking and we become irrational. We function more under our physical and emotional brains. We equally become very idealistic. We start thinking in the following manner: _"If I can get this result, it will solve all my problems and my life would move forward. But if I don't get this result, then there is nothing else I can do that would move my life forward."_ We see the problem as a major obstacle that must be "removed" for our work to go forward, for us to achieve our goals.

That's how the hiring manager thinks when they have a pressing problem to solve.

So, get inside your prospective hiring manager's head. Get into their reality. Experience what they are experiencing. Ask yourself…What is the problem? What is the pain? What is the burning desire? And most importantly, what do they think is the solution? (Here's where they start becoming idealistic – they "cling" to one idea of a solution or results – and it's critical that you know this "solution idea" of theirs.)

How is the problem getting worse? How are they trying to solve it? Is their solution making it worse?

Then ask yourself... what is it that they think is the "magic" solution? And finally, what can you propose that fits that solution or is an extension of what they think they need?

An example of how I "got into the head" of my prospective hiring manager – the CEO, after doing my gold-digging research and situational assessment, is shown in the document entitled:

"FearsFrustrationsGoalsChallenges-PotterExpressCo."

Download and take a careful look at it.

After you've finished doing your "perspectiving" (or thinking from the hiring manager's perspective), start brainstorming and researching for a solution.

Think as if there is nothing that can stop you from finding and providing a perfect ideal solution to their problem. Use "possibility thinking." Simply say to yourself that "anything is possible." This is because our thinking is constrained by what we think is possible.

Ever heard of Robert Schuller, author of *Tough Times Never Last, But Tough People Do?*

His "possibility thinking" message makes him one of the most believable and likeable success evangelists in America. According to Robert Schuller, here's how possibility thinking works:

*"When a person begins to believe 'it just might be possible, somehow, someway, somewhere, someday' - then in that magic moment of possibility thinking, three miracles occur:*

*1. Opportunity-spotting brain cells activate! 2. Problem-solving brain cells come to life 3. Determination-energizing chemicals are released into their blood stream!"*

Follow this method of possibility thinking with an open mind to possibilities for a solution. I guarantee you, if you stick to it for a while, you'll get headway toward a solution. Then, imagine how the solution translates into tangible cash for you and see how you can provide it to them.

If you do this, the answer you get will be priceless – it will be worth a high-paying job for you.

In my case, I had to carefully research my prospect's needs by asking the gold-digging research questions we saw in Step 2. I used those same techniques and interviewed some key employees who were working there.

Then, I put the pieces of information I got together and saw how they fit together - and how they were affecting the life of the CEO.

Next, I did some research on the subject of purchasing, supply management, and truck maintenance, coupled with what I already knew from my experience. I also got into my SPSM certification course notes and pulled out some killer solution ideas.

Then finally, I described the solution in the words that my prospect would most likely use to think and talk about their problems. That created the "magic" solution.

So, what can you do in your case?

Can you interview some key people working in your target companies, using the powerful gold digging and situational assessment questions we saw previously? Can you take an online short course to adjust your skills and find answers to your prospect's problems? Is there something good you know you're doing in your company that your colleagues or competitors in your target companies are not doing? Are there some common mistakes your colleagues of the same profession, who are working in other companies, are making that you have a better approach for? Is there a transfer of competence you can make from your present industry to the industry of your targeted companies?

The possibilities are endless. You just need to think.

For example, if you are a practicing lawyer in a law firm, can you apply your expertise to the legal department of a Fortune 500 company, for a lucrative position of Legal Advisor or Independent Legal Consultant? Or, if you are a nursing professional, can you apply to work in the first aid or emergency service unit of a high-risk manufacturing company for a higher than normal pay? Again, the possibilities are endless.

These are all questions and good opportunity areas to explore. The price of doing all these is less than 3% of the payoff in high salary, benefits and lifestyle, a high-paying job can offer you. Think about that.

Here's another possibility: Can you interview some well-known experts on the subject matter and "pick their brains" on what would be a great solution to your prospect's problem? Remember, if you are hired as a manager, you may in turn bring in the experts you interviewed as consultants to solve the problem. This is all part of your problem solving skills. You must not be the one to execute the solution – you are rather being paid for the solution you suggested and orchestrated.

Make sure the final result you propose in your 3MM is specific, measurable, physical, observable and tangible. People generally want results that can be expressed out-there-in-the-world, so anyone can see. For example: *"I'll help you double your productivity... so that you'll increase customer satisfaction by 60%."*


# RULE OF INFLUENCE #2: Powerful Persuasion Is An "Unconscious Process"

Action comes after emotion.

Find out, using one or more sets of gold-digging questions, the "moving-away-from" and "moving-towards" motivators, which can get your prospect out of their "comfort zone" *automatically* and *unconsciously*. Then, speak to those motivators – twice as many times to the "moving-away-from" motivators as to the "moving-towards" motivators.

Make a list of the top fears, frustrations, challenges and goals of your prospective hiring manager. Put a star on them. Make sure you find out and include those that are highly motivating to your list. People can only take action while they are out of their comfort zone – caused by a top-priority problem to solve.

Among your starred fears, frustrations, goals and challenges (see the "FearsFrustrationsGoalsChallenges-PotterExpressCo." document for an example), look for the strong motivators and underline them. Then "speak" *smoothly* and *directly* to these motivators (or "emotional hot buttons," as they are commonly called), in a way that would move the prospect to action.

You are not doing anything ethically wrong. You are simply influencing your prospect to make the right decision and solve their problems by hiring you. There's a big difference between pushing somebody to do something in their benefit and trying to flat-out rip them off. We humans are hard-core procrastinators, and so we need an over-dose of motivation…positive or negative… to act. Simply consider this a win-win. Help them do the right thing to get their own needs met. Help them hire you to solve their problem.

Here is a lesson from John Carlton, one of the world's greatest Direct Response Marketing and Advertizing Copywriters: *"The hardest thing to do - the hardest skill to learn, is how to make the 'human animal' to take out their wallet and give you their money."*

(Note: For your information, "Direct Response Marketing" is the form of marketing where you contact a prospect directly through a sales letter or other medium of communication in a way that influences them to "respond" to your communication. That is the principle we are using here. The techniques of Direct Response Marketing have been field-tested and refined for over 100 years. Direct Response Marketing, unlike Brand Marketing, whose results cannot be measured, has finally become a *near-exact* science with very predictable and measurable results.)

Although it's the company's "wallet" we're involved with here, somebody has to make the decision to take money out of that wallet to pay as a salary to hire you. That person or hiring decision maker needs to be motivated to do so.

Why is this so?

We are programmed that money is EVERYTHING – that money is life. As my marketing coach, Eben Pagan, says, *"We consider money as bio-survival tickets."*

So, what do all these mean? And how could you use these important facts in your 3MM?

Once again, take a look at the "FearsFrustrationsGoalsChallenges-PotterExpressCo." document and see how the top fears, frustrations, challenges and goals of the CEO of Potter Express Co. were *starred* and *underlined*. Also see how those emotional hot buttons or irrational motivators were targeted and "smacked upon" in the *headline* of the "Potter Express 3MM", which says:

*"3 Most DANGEROUS And HIGH-COST Mistakes You Are Probably Making While Managing Your Transportation Business… That Might Wickedly Slash-down Your Profits & Cash Flow, STOP You From Paying Back Your Bank Loan, And Cause A DISASTROUS Loss of Your Banker's Confidence Forever… And How To Avoid Them."*

Then, in Paragraph 11: *"If you really want to reduce your maintenance costs and increase your profits and cash flow…in a way that would allow you to meet your monthly loan repayments and avoid losing the great confidence your banker has in you, then…"*

Then, in Paragraph 18: *"And given the importance of you meeting your payment obligations to the bank, this is certainly one of the WORST things you want to have going on with your business."*

Paragraph 19: *"You see, if your banker loses confidence in you... caused by the fact that you can no longer respect your promises, for whatever reason... they might confiscate your trucks. And that alone can FORCE your company out of business and eventually cause you to lose your job."*

Paragraph 30: *"This may get in the way of your objectives and efforts of getting all spending under control... so that you maximize your profits, respect your monthly loan repayment obligations and avoid losing the confidence of your banker."*

Paragraph 34: *"If you don't have a good negotiator on your team, you can be sure that you are very far from having great deals. And this might make it practically impossible for you to make enough profits and cash flow to pay your loans and avoid losing your banker's confidence in you."*

Paragraph 52: *"My research, knowledge and experience have helped me develop some special skills that can REALLY help you maximize your profits and cash flow... in a way that will not only enable you to meet your monthly loan repayment, but help you WIN your banker's full confidence."*

And some more paragraphs like these you may discover by yourself in the 3MM report.

## RULE OF INFLUENCE #3: People Are Moved Twice As Much By *Moving-Away-From* Motivators As By *Moving-Towards* Motivators

For people to be moved by moving-towards motivation, it has to be a very strong form of motivation.

For example, with most hiring managers, the fear of being fired is stronger than the desire of being promoted.

So, when communicating with a prospective hiring manager, to influence him/her to offer you a high-paying job (the type of job that would offer you a *success-sized salary* to help you pay part of your debt and live a better life), you'd need to use twice as many moving-away-from motivators as moving-towards motivators.

So, agitate and "pump up" the *moving-away-from motivators* by explaining to them why the situation may be worse than what they think. Show them the dangerous consequences if they don't take action. This is a great way to help them solve their problems – by influencing them to hire you. This is what is known as powerful communication – communication that makes people take action.

So, why is the *3 Mistakes Marketing* technique so appropriate for agitating and pumping up *moving-away-from* motivation in your prospective hiring manager's mind? And how did I apply this rule to my 3MM?

Let me explain:

First, the 3MM technique is based on highlighting some of the most *dangerous mistakes* that your prospect is making as they try to solve their major problems. Your prospective hiring manager, who is in need of a solution, typically feels unstable already. So, this is naturally the most favorable moment to suggest some mistakes they are making – in this case, 3 most dangerous (or critical) mistakes. And most importantly, it helps you demonstrate your competence in advance.

Now, no matter the field you are involved in, if you cannot suggest 3 mistakes to a prospective hiring manager, then, not only you do not merit getting hired, but you might as well not need reading this book further. Why not simply return the book and ask for a refund of your money, because I believe that pointing out 3 mistakes to a prospective hiring manager is one of the simplest things ANYONE can do. Right?

Second, each mistake helps to explain and amplify their moving-away-from motivators. See paragraphs 13, 14, 15, 17, 19, 22 and 29 for example (I have underlined the lines that describe and invoke the moving-away-from motivators that force the prospect to act):

Paragraph 13: *"You know, when you don't have all your maintenance services and replacement parts being handled by one specific contractor, like in the case of contract-based maintenance services, it makes it difficult for the contractor to properly plan for your needs. And so, they don't make provisions for the type of replacement parts your trucks need, well in advance and at low cost."*

Paragraph 14: *"Result? They are always placing rush overseas orders for replacement parts in order to catch up with maintenance and repairs of your trucks. And this makes the cost of maintenance SKYROCKET."*

Paragraph 15: *"Another problem is that, since none of your different contractors have all or a greater portion of your truck maintenance business to handle, within the framework of a contract, they CANNOT offer you their best prices, as they'd normally do for most of their important customers."*

Paragraph 17: *"As you can see, you MUST be losing a LARGE amount of money, especially taking into consideration the size of your fleet of trucks."*

Paragraph 18: *"And given the importance of you meeting your payment obligations to the bank, this is certainly one of the WORST things you want to have going on with your business."*

Paragraph 19: *"You see, if your banker loses confidence in you… because you can no longer respect your promises, for whatever reason… they might confiscate your trucks. And that alone can FORCE your Company out of business and eventually cause you to lose your job."*

Paragraph 22: *"So what is a good Savings Strategy? And why is not having one for your business a BIG, BIG MISTAKE?"*

Paragraph 29: *"Imagine that, because of quality and other 'selfish' reasons an experienced contractor might give you; you end up having 'hidden costs' that will end up blowing your maintenance cost through the roof."*

These and more such paragraphs you may discover by yourself in the 3MM document, including the headline itself.

## RULE OF INFLUENCE #4: Communicate Using The Four Basic Learning Styles

According to David Kolb, a Professor of Organizational Behavior at Case Western Reserve University, who earned his Ph.D. from Harvard, people generally assimilate information through four learning styles.

Simply put, you have: "What learners," "Why learners," "What-if learners," and "How learners".

1.  The **"What learners"** want you to set up the context, define the problem and state the facts. They also want to get the theory and high-level concepts of the solution. They want some examples, illustrations, statistics or test results.

2.  The **"Why learners"** want to be motivated to learn. They want to know the reason why they should listen to you. Or the pain, dangers, advantages, and consequences of taking or not taking your advice.

3.  The **"What-if learners"** want to know the pay-off or what will happen if they go and apply or take action on the solution you are suggesting. They have a strong preference for doing and getting results rather than thinking.

4.  The **"How learners"** want the "action steps" or step-by-step process to get to the solution of the problem.

Note: We all prefer all four learning styles, but to varying degrees.

Bottom line: When communicating, make sure you respect the needs of all four learning styles in your communication. This will maximize your chances of being understood.

As Wyatt Woodsmall rightly says, *"If you can describe another person's problem better than they can, they automatically assume you know the solution."*

Here's how to use the 4-learning-styles of communication with your 3MM:

1.  Use the "What" and "Why" style communication a lot, to heat up the *moving-away-from* and *moving-towards* motivation, as well as the curiosity, of the hiring manager.

2.  And while the hiring manager is fired up and out of their comfort zone, and is expecting a solution, then you use the "What-if" (in other words, the payoff, if they take action and hire you) and finally, the "How" (the step-by-step process to get to the solution, which includes contacting you to discuss the next steps).

This is how you use the 4 learning styles of effective communication to "push" the hiring manager or decision maker into hiring you solve their problems.

Let's see some examples of these from my 3MM.

**Examples of "What learners" style communication - the "What":**

In Paragraph 7 : *"Mistake #1: Thinking of having a Client Account & Fleet Manager without a Truck Maintenance Contract, with Negotiated Fixed Prices."*

Paragraph 8: *"I understand that... when you have such an important contract to deliver, the first and logical thing to do is to look for someone to look after the management of the trucks, to make sure they are properly maintained, so that the client would always have trucks available to transport their products safely and on time."*

Paragraph 9: *"This is a GREAT way to look at the solution to the problem."*

Paragraph 10: *"BUT, there is more to it than that."*

Paragraph 11: *"If you really want to reduce your maintenance costs and increase your profits and cash flow…in a way that would allow you to meet your monthly loan repayments and avoid losing the great confidence your banker has in you, then…"*

Part-1 of Paragraph 12: *"…You also need to have a truck maintenance contract with pre-negotiated truck maintenance prices…"*

Paragraph 16: *"In a calculation we did with one company, whom I advised to switch from six maintenance contractors to one single contractor with a well negotiated contract, we found that they were initially spending on maintenance up to 30 cents out of every dollar they made as gross profits after deducting direct operations costs. And after putting in place a contract, they were spending ONLY 10 cents out of every dollar they got as gross profits. They made a savings of 20 cents per dollar on maintenance costs and that increased their profits by 20 cents per dollar as well as their cash flow."*

Paragraph 17: *"As you can see, you MUST be losing a LARGE amount of money, especially taking into consideration the size of your fleet of trucks."*

Paragraph 18: *"And given the importance of you meeting your payment obligations to the bank, this is certainly one of the WORST things you want to have going on with your business."*

Paragraph 19: *"You see, if your banker loses confidence in you… because you can no longer respect your promises, for whatever reason… they might confiscate your trucks. And that alone can FORCE your company out of business and eventually cause you to lose your job."*

Paragraph 21: *"Mistake #2: Not having a well-defined, well-developed and carefully-executed Savings Strategy in place."*

Paragraph 31: *"Mistake N#3: Not Having a Powerful and Professional Negotiator on Your Team.*

Paragraph 32: *"When it comes to REALLY succeeding in having the best prices from your contractors, a powerful and professional negotiator is KEY."*

Paragraph 34: *"If you don't have a good negotiator in your team, you can be sure that you are very far from having great deals. And this might make it practically impossible for you to make enough profits and cash flow to pay your loans and avoid losing your banker's confidence in you."*

## Examples of "Why learners" style communication - the "Why":

Part-2 of Paragraph 12: *"...This will not only ensure you have a well defined budget on truck maintenance to stick to, but you'll also benefit from low prices."*

(As you can see, 'what' and 'why' communication can be linked in one paragraph as in the case of part-1 and part-2 of paragraph 12. In fact, 'what' and 'why' communication are, most of the time, interwoven.)

Paragraph 13: *"You know, when you don't have all your maintenance services and replacement parts being handled by one specific contractor, like in the case of contract-based maintenance services, it makes it difficult for the contractor to properly plan for your needs. And so, they don't make provisions for the type of replacement parts your trucks need, well in advance and at low cost."*

Paragraph 14: *"Result? They are always placing rush overseas orders for replacement parts in order to catch up with maintenance and repairs of your trucks. And this makes the cost of maintenance SKYROCKET."*

Paragraph 15: *"Another problem is that, since none of your different contractors have all or a greater portion of your truck maintenance business to handle, within the framework of a contract, they CANNOT offer you their best prices, as they'd normally do for most of their important customers."*

Paragraph 22: *"So, what is a good Savings Strategy? And <u>why</u> is not having one for your business a BIG, BIG MISTAKE?"*

Paragraph 23: *"Well, here are four big things a great savings strategy CAN and MUST achieve:"*

Paragraph 24: *"First, it gives you a clear and detailed idea of what your company is spending on every item for truck maintenance – from replacement parts to routine and regular inspections, servicing and repairs."*

Paragraph 25: *"Second, it enables you to package and communicate your maintenance workload to your contractors…in a way that makes them see how big and lucrative your maintenance business could be for them. In other words, you want them to feel the need to compete for your business and offer you low and competitive prices."*

Paragraph 26: *"Third, it gives you a starting point from which to measure your progress, after putting a contract in place."*

Paragraph 27: *"Fourth, it helps you know how good a deal the best contractor is offering you."*

Paragraph 33: *"A good negotiator will help you handle some of the most closely-kept negotiation secrets most contractors don't want you to know."*

**Examples of "What-if learners" style communication - the "What-if"**

(See underlined sentences for the "pay offs" the prospect will get if they take action – the non-underlined parts contain either "what", "why" or "how" communication):

Paragraph 52: *"My research, knowledge and experience have helped me develop some special skills that <u>can REALLY help you maximize your profits and cash flow</u>… in a way that will not only <u>enable you to meet your monthly loan repayment</u>, but will <u>help you WIN your banker's full confidence</u>."*

Paragraph 53: *"Here are the special skills I have developed that I can directly put to work for you:"*

Paragraph 54: -> *How to "lock in" negotiated pricing, service delivery specifications, and warranties that FORCE a contractor to deliver the best price, service and quality, EVERY MONTH.*

Paragraph 55: -> *How to avoid poor contractor service that causes truck breakdowns and financial penalties from customers, which make it unlikely to meet monthly loan payments.*

Paragraph 56: -> *Certified contract-writing techniques to protect your company from risks – like being "legally committed" to a poor performing, high-cost contractor for years (causing low profits and cash flow and failure to meet loan repayments)*

Paragraph 57: ->*A "Systematic Method" of identifying, analyzing and executing cost avoidance and savings opportunities that automatically maximize total monthly savings, boosts profits and cash flow and enables repayment of loans and other financial obligations.*

Paragraph 58: *"-> My 4-step "bonding-with-the-team" formula for building STRONG working "bonds" with any team... that facilitates working and learning - VITAL to achieving ANY goal."*

Paragraph 59: -> *Closely-kept negotiation secrets contractors don't want you to know (how to use them to get the best deals reserved only for savvy buyers and best customers).*

Paragraph 60: -> *And much, much, more.*

## Examples of "How learners" style communication – the "How"

(See underlined sentences for the "action steps" the prospect is required to take – the non-underlined parts contain either "what", "why" or "what-if" communication):

Paragraph 61: *"Let me know how I can start offering my help to you and your business, so that you will not only be able to satisfy your customer and boost your profits & cash flow, but you'll also be able to secure payments of your loan and become the type of customer your banker will always like to do business with."*

Paragraph 62: *"If you have any questions or would like us to discuss this further, please contact me."*

Paragraph 65: *"P.S: Again... if you really want to reduce your maintenance costs and increase your profits and cash flow...in a way that would allow you to meet your monthly loan repayments and avoid losing the great confidence your banker has in you, then now is the time to act, especially now that I am available and ready to help. Simply call me at: 1 641 980 5516 or email me at Slyn2012@gmail.com"*

# RULE OF INFLUENCE #5: Use 100-Dollar Words

The only difference between a *1 dollar bill* and a *100 dollar bill* is the message printed on them. They are both paper with images printed on them. But the imaginary and emotional meanings and values attached to those images are *enormously* different.

The same goes with words. When you use hundred-dollar words, you get hundred-dollar responses. Most of the words we use are 1- dollar words. They are not really valuable or compelling.

If John Carlton, the famous and great copywriter, was to describe a 1-dollar word, he would say: *"1-dollar words do not carry an emotional wallop."*

Example: Compare the words "increased" and "boosted" as used in the following phrases: "increased sales" and "boosted sales."

The phrases "increased sales" and "boosted sales" all have the same intellectual meaning (just as a 1-dollar and a 100-dollar bill are both printed on paper), but different emotional impact and value. The phrase *"boosted* sales" is more emotionally loaded than the phrase *"increased* sales."

Compare these two headlines and see which one is more powerful. Take note of the 1-dollar and 100-dollar words:

*"3 Most COMMON And COSTLY Mistakes You Are Probably Making While Managing Your Transportation Business... That Might Seriously Reduce Your Profits & Cash Flow, PREVENT You From Paying Back Your Bank Loan, And Cause An UNDESIRABLE Loss of Your Banker's Confidence Forever... And How To Avoid Them."*

*--VS--*

*"3 Most DANGEROUS And HIGH-COST Mistakes You Are Probably Making While Managing Your Transportation Business... That Might Wickedly Slash-down Your Profits & Cash Flow, STOP You From Paying Back Your Bank Loan, And Cause A DISASTROUS Loss of Your Banker's Confidence Forever... And How To Avoid Them."*

Which headline carries the most 100-dollar words?

I guess you'd say all the underlined words in the *second headline* are a hundred times more emotional than those in the first. You're right. They are 100-dollar words. And they are worth a lot of money.

# RULE OF INFLUENCE #6: Use Crystal Clear and Powerful Communication

Your communication will be crystal clear and powerful when you follow the following rules:

1. **Make everything anchored to the real world**. Everything should be tangible, specific, external, and measurable. Avoid abstract and big words. Write in a way that a first grade child would understand. Use short words and explain everything to avoid the possibility of misunderstanding. Do everything you can, to drive away confusion and ambiguity out of your statements and sentences.

2. **Start with a "bang" or high tone**. Startle your prospect to capture and "plug in" their attention. Use attention-grabbing headlines that speak about the major moving-away-from and moving-towards motivators of the prospect.

3. **Speak-write**. Write to your prospect in the same way you'd speak to them if you were in a room with them, one-on-one. Visualize or imagine that you are speaking to them one-on-one and write as you speak. When addressing the prospective hiring manager or hiring decision maker or whoever the target is, use "you". Speak as if you are talking just to one person directly. That's what I mean by speak-write.

4. **Put the stage-lights on the prospective hiring manager's needs**. Talk about what's in it for them. Even when you talk about yourself, make sure it's in direct relation to their needs.

5. **Use examples and stories** to drive home your points.

My 3MM report was written following all the crystal clear communication guidelines described here. Take your time and really go through it, as many times as you can, to really learn from it.

Even this entire Job-getting Formula book is written following the same rules of crystal-clear communication.

# RULE OF INFLUENCE #7: Use The Reciprocation Weapon

If you want something, you first need to give something.

People will always feel indebted to someone who has done them a favor, no matter how small the favor may be, and no matter whether the favor was requested or not.

Moreover, human nature considers it impolite and makes it extremely difficult (if not practically impossible) to turn down uninvited favors, not only because we think the person doing the favor has invested time and money, but because we somehow feel deeply uncomfortable turning down a free gift.

Think of all the people you have responded positively to because they did something good to you. For example, they greeted you and asked you *"What time is it?"* How happily and nicely did you respond?

Think about how many times you've received small uninvited gifts through the mail, such as personalized greeting cards, gadgets, free product information kits, DVDs – either from charity agencies that ask for funds in an attached note, or from companies that would later on ask you to buy if you liked the free report, gadget, DVD or other free gift.

Did you willingly turn down the free gift or did you open it up and check it out? Even if you later on dumped it in the trash because it wasn't particularly interesting to you, you wouldn't want the senders of the gift to know that that's what you did. Right?

Now think about a gift that carefully matched your needs. What did you do with it? Did you use it? Of course, yes!

So, if you want to create a relationship with your prospective hiring manager, give them something for free that matches their moving-away-from and moving-towards motivators, as discovered through your gold-digging research. Share with them some little secret or cutting-edge technique that can help them solve their problems. This is the same principle the 3MM technique is based on.

Teach and you shall receive. Share useful knowledge with your prospective hiring manager, in the form of 3 mistakes. This is a stunningly tremendous way to show that you are skillful, knowledgeable, experienced and dedicated to service.

It sets you apart from the crowd. It shows you can go the extra mile to achieve results more than you are paid for. The proof is: you are offering FREE and superior service with your 3MM report without asking for pay. It's like indebting the hiring manager with your services, in a way that they're not even conscious of.

Looking at it from a different angle, you are exploiting the strong "cultural pressure" all humans feel to reciprocate a gift to work in your favor, in the form of a trusted relationship, which will most probably lead to the hiring manager calling you for an interview. Awesome indeed! It instantly helps you to build a trustful and credible relationship.

If you think of it, the entire "3 Mistakes Marketing™" technique, in itself, is an example of (and is based on) how to use the sneakily powerful weapon of reciprocation, to painlessly get the attention of *any* hiring manager and build a working relationship that eventually gets you the high-paying job you want. In a friendly manner, you are *skillfully* pin-pointing the dangerous mistakes of the prospective hiring manager. They can only feel grateful to you for doing so. And the payoffs are often unbelievable.

# RULE OF INFLUENCE #8: Use The "Commitment And Consistency" Weapon

If you can get people to commit to something small, you can get them to commit to something big. This is an astonishingly simple but powerful influence weapon used by people who are masters of the psychology of persuasion.

If you can carefully describe the problem your prospective hiring manager is facing, and ask them if they agree with you that that's the problem they are facing – and they respond "yes"... then they'll equally respond "yes" if you ask them if they want a solution for that problem. And they'll most likely answer yes, if you ask them if they'll be willing to invite you for an interview or hire you to solve that problem.

This is the weapon of commitment and consistency in action.

People will do everything to be consistent with their identity and self-image. They want to keep to their words.

Let me show you how to activate this "dangerous" weapon in your 3MM.

Consider the following paragraphs, and observe how they successfully get the CEO to answer YES and commit to what I was about to say. These are facts I gathered from my gold-digging and situational assessment research, expressed in the form of questions, which I knew they MUST answer "yes" to:

Paragraph 3: *"Has Your Company just won a new transportation contract that requires new trucks to deliver?"*

Paragraph 4: *"Have you acquired new trucks with the help of a bank loan to deliver great quality transportation services to your client?"*

Paragraph 5: *"Are you afraid that, because the lucrative nature of this contract is challenged by the large number of new trucks to effectively manage, you might not have enough cash flow at the end of the month to pay back the loan?"*

And then, see how I got him to consistently commit to the fact that, they are "probably" making the 3 mistakes, with the following follow-up phrase:

Paragraph 6: *"If you answer yes to these questions, then you are probably making one or more of these 3 mistakes:"*

Also see how commitment and consistency was use in the final call to action:

Paragraph 65: *"P.S: Again… if you really want to reduce your maintenance costs and increase your profits and cash flow…in a way that would allow you to meet your monthly loan repayments and avoid losing the great confidence your banker has in you, then now is the time to act, especially now that I am available and ready to help. Simply call me at: 1 641 980 5516 or email me at slyn2012@gmail.com"*

This is like saying to the hiring manager that, if you agree that you have [*these* "emotional hot button" *problems*] and really want [*these* "emotional hot button" *results*], then take action now (or are you willing to take action now?)

# RULE OF INFLUENCE #9: Use The Social Proof Weapon

When we are having difficulty in making a choice, what do we do? Most often, we look around, see what other people are doing, then copy them. That's a behavior all of us are *wired* with. It's part of our decision making system, as humans. This type of behavior is called social proof or group behavior.

Example: Think of how people respond to posted comments on Facebook. You may realize that the group always follows a particular trend that was introduced by the first people who commented on the post. If most people like the post, there is a higher tendency of other people liking it. If the first people commented positively, the rest of the people will equally comment positively.

Another example is when you get into a strange town to find a restaurant. Let's say you find two restaurants close to each other. One has lots of cars in its parking lot, while the other has one or two cars. Which restaurant would you choose? If you are like most people, you'd likely check out the one with lots of cars. Right? That's using social proof (or group behavior) to make a decision.

In the same way, if a hiring manager sees that some other people are already saying great things about you, it will automatically cause them to trust you. You can use this power of social proof in the form of adding testimonials and recommendations on your résumé, cover letter, and 3MM report. You can get them from other people like your boss, colleagues, boss' boss, happy customers, etc.

Here are examples of how this rule was implemented in my 3MM.

First, just below and related to, the achievement in Paragraph 49:

*"(The Managing Director lauded the teamwork and professionalism demonstrated throughout the project, which enabled the company to cope with inflated transportation costs, due to an increase in fuel prices and shortage of fit-for-the-road trucks, coupled with a tight budget.)"*

Second, just below and related to, the achievement in paragraph 50:

*"(After working on the tendering and contracting process for CCTV – Closed Circuit Television System, the Security Manager, who was the major stakeholder, sent me the following recognition in an email:*

*'The professionalism with which you have handled the CCTV bid package is testament of your mastery of best practice. Keep it up!')"*

Third, just after the two selected achievements, and talking about both of them:

*"These achievements earned me a Recognition Certificate from my boss that says:"*

"Dear Sylvester Nkongho,

I personally want to acknowledge your input and contribution among the procurement team.

Thank you for the overall success of GCSA in F08,

I wish you all the best for F09.

Head of Procurement

J. N."

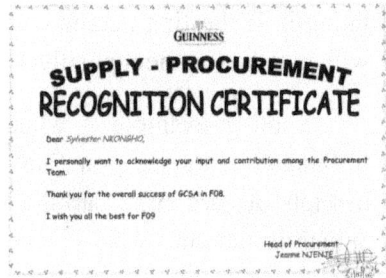

# RULE OF INFLUENCE #10: Use The Authority Weapon

We have been conditioned for ages to respect authority, starting from our parents, to our teachers, medical doctors, government officials, and public institutions like schools, colleges and universities, as well as the media like: TV, radio, newspaper, etc. All these entities can be referred to as "authority figures."

In order to get a high-paying job, you want to use the power of an "authority figure" in your field to prove that you are a good and credible choice.

For example, let's say you received a special award, a Special Recognition, an MBA, or certification from a person of authority or an institution that's considered an authority in your field. That alone will greatly influence the hiring decision of your prospective hiring manager, in your favor.

If you did a project that was spoken about on national TV, radio, newspaper, or magazine - include images of it in your 3MM, cover letter and résumé. The TV, radio, newspaper and magazines are also Authority media. There are many ways you can showcase authority endorsement. Just look around you and you'll start discovering them.

Here's how I applied this rule in my 3MM.

Just after paragraph 47:

*"And I also became SPSM certified. Here's the SPSM Certification I earned:"*

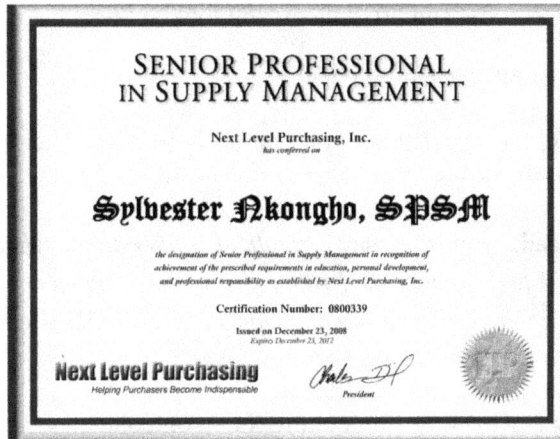

Remember, I had previously said in paragraph 43 that:

*"And as if by luck, I stumbled on one of the <u>world's leading online certification courses in purchasing and supply management</u>. It was the <u>SPSM certification</u> – <u>Senior Professional in Supply Management</u>, offered by <u>Next Level Purchasing Inc.</u>"*

That's where the authority came from – the underlined phrases.

# RULE OF INFLUENCE #11: Use The "Liking" Weapon

People like to work or do business with people they perceive as being like them. They like people who think like them.

Build rapport with your prospect and lead them with your solution from their own perspective.

Get this straight:

When someone is desperately trying to solve an important problem, and they feel like they are making a mistake, or they think they are in trouble and everything is going the wrong way... they don't want someone to come and "fix" them, and look at them as the problem.

That's NOT what they want.

Now, the worst thing you can do is to come and say *"Hey, you're getting it all wrong..."*

Instead, you can say *"yeah, I understand what you're going through. I feel your pain. I think you're heading in the right direction, but here's where you're making a mistake and this is what you must do, or need to get done, to see better results..."*

This is what they are looking for – someone they can trust. Someone who can readily recognize and applaud the efforts they are making. They're not just going to be interested in anything you have to say, until they know you're that person that they can trust.

So the insight here is, you have to first build rapport and trust with your prospect, before proposing your solution… because the feeling of "feeling understood" is one of the rarest and one of the most valuable a human being can, and wants to have from others.

This simple weapon of Liking or Rapport is like relationship magic. It's like relationship voodoo or relationship super-powers – or whatever you want me to call it. But it works like magic to build trust.

If you use it well, you'll become a good and trusted friend. If you mess with it, you're tossed and your prospect won't want to hear anything more from you.

Here's an example from my 3MM report.

Paragraphs 7 to 10:

*"Mistake #1: Thinking of having a Client Account & Fleet Manager without having a Truck Maintenance Contract with Negotiated Fixed Prices.*

*I understand that… when you have such an important contract to deliver, the first and logical thing to do is to look for someone to look after the management of the trucks to make sure they are properly maintained, so that the client would always have trucks available to transport their products safely and on time.*

*This is a GREAT way to look at the solution to the problem.*

*BUT, there is more to it than that."*

First, notice how mistake #1 is *carefully* phrased. It highlights the CEO's intention of hiring a *Client Account & Fleet Manager* (the phrase: *"Thinking of having a Client Account & Fleet Manager…"*).

This is thinking from the CEO's perspective. Then it "connects" their way of looking at the problem to the mistake they are making (with the continuation phrase: *"…without having a Truck Maintenance Contract with Negotiated Fixed Prices."*)

This is how you build rapport at the start of your conversation with a "kind reframe" of the 3 mistakes – in this particular case, Mistake #1.

Then, it continues with the phrase, *"I understand that...".* This is what gives the hiring manager the impression that you understand the efforts they are already putting in to solve the problem.


### Rapport-building Story – A Step Further In Building Rapport

This actually has to do with showing proof that you understand the situation and problem your prospect is in. You do this by sharing a story of you having been in a similar situation.

Just saying *"I understand what you're going through. I feel your pain..."* may not be sufficient to convince your prospect. You may then need to demonstrate through a story that you've been involved in a similar, near-similar or worse situation.

When speaking about yourself to your prospective hiring manager, talk mostly, and if possible, only about elements that you share in common. When sharing your story, look for those elements of your story that overlap with the problems, the nature and the situation of your prospective hiring manager. Use the same words they'll use in describing their problems.

The truth is that the hiring manager doesn't care a bit about you, your experience and your skills. All they care about is themselves and their problems.

Let me show you how to use this simple but powerful rapport-building story weapon in your 3MM, to build rapport and a good relationship with your prospective hiring manager... in a way that will force them to call you for an interview and probably hire you.

First, you need a story of how you came about with the solution you want to provide to your prospect. The psychological premise in the prospect's mind is that, if you got a solution, then you must have the specific details of how you came about it.

For example, my story kicks off in paragraph 35, with the following phrase:

*"So how do I know all this? And why should you listen to me?"*

But there are some "killer ingredients" your story must have for it to build instant rapport, trust and credibility. Make sure you tell your story in a way that clearly exposes these ingredients:

1. **Starting Point or Situation:** Where you were when you first started, or how you got involved in a similar or even worse situation or problem.

2. **How You Tried & Failed:** Emotionally persuasive true story of trying and failing.

3. **The Breakthrough Moment:** How you learned something that "miraculously" worked.

4. **Results Achieved**: The results you got with other employers.

5. **Skills Developed And How They Can Help Your Prospect:** The special skills you have developed that you can directly put to work to help your prospective hiring manager achieve results.

Here's how these ingredients were applied to my 3MM.

## 1. **Starting Point or Situation (example):**

Paragraph 36: *"A few years ago, my previous employer was involved in a serious business crisis where we were not making any profits AT ALL, for a period of six months, caused by a big and aggressive nationwide marketing promotion of our leading competitor - who owned more than 80 percent of the market."*

Paragraph 37: *"Their aim was to 'kick' us out of business."*

Paragraph 38: *"Cash flow was a pretty tough problem. We were receiving subvention in the form of loans from one of our sister companies in order to survive."*

Paragraph 39: *"So, in order to turn things around, management was supposed to implement stringent budgetary cuts accompanied by companywide cost reduction and savings projects."*

Paragraph 40: *"And being a key member of the purchasing department, I was asked by my boss to champion most of the savings and cost reduction initiatives."*

## 2. How You Tried & Failed (example):

Paragraph 41: *"I knew very little about purchasing. And coupled with the great challenges the company was facing, I was forced to do something fast and accurate in order to live up to my boss' and company's expectations. Judging from my results at work, I realized if I continued struggling with the little I knew, I was bound to keep failing, no matter how hard I tried."*

Paragraph 42: *"So I started researching and reading everything I could find about purchasing."*

## 3. The Breakthrough Moment (example):

Paragraph 43: *"And as if by luck, I stumbled on one of the world's leading online certification courses in purchasing and supply management. It was the SPSM certification – Senior Professional in Supply Management, offered by Next Level Purchasing, Inc."*

Paragraph 44: *"I immediately enrolled in the course. It was a great course – jam-packed with the most leading-edge techniques in purchasing and supply management."*

Paragraph 45: *"And I studied every subject they taught, such as Supply Management Contract Writing, Savings Strategy Development, Negotiation No-No's, Expert Purchasing Management, Executing a Global Sourcing Strategy, 14 Purchasing Best Practices, Microsoft Project for Purchasing Professionals and Microsoft Excel for Purchasing Professionals."*

Paragraph 46: *"Then, I applied what I learned from it to my job on a day-to-day, activity-to-activity, and project-by-project basis."*

Paragraph 47: *"After practicing at length with the certified techniques, I finally got a thorough understanding and mastery of almost all of them."*

## 4. Results Achieved (example):

Paragraph 48: *"And at the end of the year, I achieved the following results:"*

Paragraph 49: *"***Negotiated within budget, a $5.5 million Road Transportation Services project, by re-selecting competent Road Transportation Contractors, negotiating down prices, and establishing a 3-year contract. (October 2008 - April 2009) ***"*

Paragraph 50: *"***Saved over $250,000 by developing and implementing savings and cost avoidance strategies on major purchase categories such as Logistics and Distribution Services, Machine Spare Parts, Site Construction & Engineering Services (including CCTV), Cleaning, and General Support Services.(July 2007 - April 2009)***"*

## 5. Skills Developed And How They Can Help Prospect (example):

Paragraph 51: *"What skills have I learned and how can they help you?"*

Paragraph 52: *"My research, knowledge and experience have helped me developed some special skills that can REALLY help you maximize your profits and cash flow... in a way that will not only enable you to meet your monthly loan repayment, but will help you WIN your banker's full confidence."*

Paragraph 53: *"Here are the special skills I have developed that I can directly put to work for you:"*

Paragraph 54: -> *"How to 'lock in' negotiated pricing, service delivery specifications, and warranties that FORCE a contractor to deliver the best price, service and quality, EVERY MONTH."*

Paragraph 55: -> *"How to avoid poor contractor service that causes truck breakdowns and financial penalties from customers - making it unlikely to meet monthly loan payments."*

And the list of skills continues from paragraph 56 to 60.

## RULE OF INFLUENCE #12: Use The Scarcity Weapon

There is nothing as appealing and attractive as a rapidly diminishing supply of what we want. We are wired to value what's in short supply. Our longing always directs its attention towards what is missing or in short supply.

How can you show your prospective hiring manager that you might be available to serve, only for a limited time? And that if they want to hire you, they need to act fast? Think about that for a moment. There are a few ways to do that.

Here's one way I used in my 3MM (for clarity, I have underlined the relevant phrase):

Paragraph 65: *P.S: Again… if you really want to reduce your maintenance costs and increase your profits and cash flow…in a way that would allow you to meet your monthly loan repayments and avoid losing the great confidence your banker has in you, <u>then now is the time to act, especially now that I am available and ready to help</u>. Simply contact me at: 1 641980 5516 or email me at Slyn2012@gmail.com.*

## RULE OF INFLUENCE #13: Use Fascination Formulas To "WOW" Your Prospect

When making a promise of results or when describing your special skills with the aim of making your prospective hiring manager take action, there is one very effective way to communicate. It is the use of fascination formulas.

Here are some examples of fascinations:

- "3 things you must do if you want to stop factory waste"

- "How to use a 5-minutes-per-day secret to build highly-collaborative teams"

- "What to do when you have a helpless shortage of manufacturing raw materials"

As you may realize, all these fascinations have 6 things in common:

1. They talk about the features, advantages and benefits of the solution you can provide, in a very compelling way.

2. They are specific, tangible and measurable.

3. They create intense curiosity. Claude C. Hopkins, author of *Scientific Advertising*, says "curiosity is one of the strongest human incentives."

4. They promise instant gratification – or simple, quick, immediate and easy results. (Remember we stated earlier at the start of *Step 3*, among the four characteristics humans share with chimps and monkeys, that humans are lovers of instant gratification.)

5. They have condensed power.

6. They are fascinating.


Here's is the **Fascination Formula**:

Fascination = Specific Benefit (moving-away-from and/or moving-towards motivators) + Instant Gratification (or simple, quick and easy results) + Intense Curiosity.

That is why when you use them in your résumé, cover letter, and 3MM, they helplessly leave the hiring manager dying to know more. And in that way, it forces them to call you for an interview.

**Warning**: When writing fascinations, focus on features, advantages and benefits that are really relevant and highly-motivating to the prospect.

Here are six common fascination formulas you can start using immediately, including examples of how I used them in my 3MM:

a. **Formula #1: How To [Move Towards Result/Move Away From Problem]**

Paragraphs 54 and 55:

*"-> How to 'lock in' negotiated pricing, service delivery specifications, and warranties that FORCE a contractor to deliver the best price, service and quality, EVERY MONTH."*

*"-> How to avoid poor contractor service that causes truck breakdowns and financial penalties from customers, which make it unlikely to meet monthly loan payments."*

b. **Formula #2: Why [Result Happens/Problem Happens]**

*"Why not having a customer service department is causing you to lose sales... And what to do about it... even if you don't want to hire somebody new"*

c. **Formula #3: What [To Do To Move Towards Result/Move Away From Problem]**

A rephrase of Paragraph 55:

*"-> What to do to avoid poor contractor service that causes truck breakdowns and financial penalties from customer, which make it unlikely to meet monthly loan payments."*

Another example:

*"What NEVER to say to a customer, if you don't want to lose them FOREVER"*

d. **Formula #4: When [To Act To Move Towards Result/Move Away From Problem]**

*"When to buy real estate without any down payment"*

e. **Formula #5: Where [To Move Towards Result/Move Away From Problem]**

*"Where to buy office stationary at 50% less than the normal market price"*

f. **Formula #6: Number Of Ways [ To Move Towards Result/Move Away From Problem]**

*"3 things you must do if you want to stop factory waste"*

g. **Formula #7: Benefit-Named Solution, Trick, Technique, or Strategy [To Move Towards Result/Move Away From Problem]**

Paragraph 58:

*"-> My 4-step 'bonding-with-the-team' formula for building STRONG working bonds with any team... that facilitates working and learning - VITAL to achieving ANY goal."*

*"7 closely-guarded Facebook marketing techniques that helped my previous employer sell 1 million dollars"*

h. **Formula #8: 3 Mistake Marketing™ Headline Formulas**

- **3** [Dangerous/Biggest/High-cost/Deadly/Critical/Etc] Mistakes That You Are Probably Making While Managing [Prospect's Business Activity]... That Might **[Cause Problems To Happen (or Worsen)]**... And How To Avoid Them

Example:

*"3 Most DANGEROUS And HIGH-COST Mistakes You Are Probably Making While Managing Your Transportation Business... That Might Wickedly <u>Slash-down Your Profits & Cash Flow</u>, STOP You From <u>Paying Back Your Bank Loan</u>, And <u>Cause A DISASTROUS Loss of Your Banker's Confidence Forever</u>... And How To Avoid Them."*

- **3** [Dangerous/Biggest/High-cost/Deadly/Critical/Etc] Mistakes To Avoid... When Trying To **[Move Towards Result/Move Away From Problem]**

Example:

*"3 Most DANGEROUS And HIGH-COST Mistakes To Avoid... When Trying To Boost <u>Your Profits & Cash Flow</u>, Meet The <u>Repayment of Your Bank Loan</u> And <u>WIN Your Banker's Confidence</u>"*

**The 4-Step Process for Writing Powerfully Condensed Fascinations:**

Here's the 4-step process for describing your skills... so that they appeal to a hiring manager's irrational motivators, make him curious, and leave him *helplessly* wanting to know more about you.

**First**, write down the *specific problem* the fascination is aimed at solving.

- Example: specific problem = "prospect is experiencing huge problem of team members not collaborating with one another"

**Second**, write down the specific technique or strategy you are offering to solve. Make sure you conceal vital details of the technique or strategy to ensure it triggers intense curiosity:

- Example: specific technique or strategy = "A 5-minutes-per-day secret"

**Third**, write down the *result or payoff* the hiring manager wants to get, in the form: *Move Towards Result or Move Away From Problem*

- Example: Result or Payoff = "build highly collaborative teams"

**Fourth**, use one of the fascination formulas above to put all three parts together.

Here are examples:

**Using Formula #1**, *"How To [Move Towards Result/Move Away From Problem]"*, we get:

- "How to use a 5-minutes-per-day secret to build highly-collaborative teams"

**Using Formula #7**, *"Benefit-Named Solution, Trick, Technique, or Strategy [To Move Towards Result/Move Away From Problem]"*, we simply get:

- "A 5-minutes-per-day secret to build highly-collaborative teams"

**Using Formula #3**, *"What [To Do To Move Towards Result/Move Away From Problem]"*, we now get:

- "What to do to build highly-collaborative teams"

When writing a marketing or sales piece, like your 3MM, your résumé and cover letter, always remember that fascinations are a form of value or currency, that you can exchange for the prospective hiring manager's own currency when they're thinking of hiring you. It is what *exponentially* maximizes the value of your knowledge, skills and experience, in the eyes of the prospect, and it sets you apart, in a unique and compelling way, from the crowd of struggling job seekers.

# The Interview-getting Résumé – What It Looks Like (This Is A Sample)

## Sly N, SPSM

San Jose, CA 95123
641-980-5516
slyn2012@gmail.com

**SUPPLY - PROCUREMENT**
**RECOGNITION CERTIFICATE**

*"Dear Sylvester Nkongho,
I personally want to
acknowledge your input and
contribution among the
procurement team.
Thank you for the overall
success of GCSA in 2008.
I wish you all the best for 2009.
--Head of Procurement, GCSA-
Diageo West Africa Hub"*

SENIOR PROFESSIONAL
IN SUPPLY MANAGEMENT

**Sylvester Nkongho, SPSM**

*"The professionalism with
which you have handled the
CCTV bid package is testament
of your mastery of best
practice. Keep it up!"
--Security Manager, GCSA-
Diageo West Africa Hub*

GUINNESS

SMIRNOFF
Johnnie Walker

DIAGEO

### Objective Summary

Help you MAXIMIZE your profits and cash flow... in a way that will not only enable you meet up with your monthly loan repayment, BUT help you WIN your banker's FULL confidence.

### Selected Accomplishments

- Negotiated within budget, a $5.5 million Road Transportation Services project, by re-selecting competent Road Transportation Contractors, negotiating down prices, and establishing a 3-year contract (October 2008 – April 2009).

- Saved over $250,000 by developing and implementing savings and cost avoidance strategies on major purchase categories such as Logistics and Distribution Services, Machine Spare parts, Site Construction & Engineering Services (including CCTV), Cleaning, and General Support Services (July 2007 – April 2009).

### Special Skills

Here are the special skills I have developed that I can directly put to work for you:

- How to "lock in" negotiated pricing, service delivery specifications, and warranties that FORCE a contractor to deliver best price, service and quality, EVERY MONTH.

- How to avoid poor contractor service that causes truck breakdowns and financial penalties from customer - making it unlikely to meet up with monthly loan payments.

- Certified contract-writing techniques to protect your Company from risks – like being "legally committed" to a poor performing, high-cost contractor for years. (causing loss of profits and cash flow and failures to meet up with loan repayments)

- A "Systematic Method" for identifying, analyzing and executing cost avoidance and savings opportunities that automatically maximizes total monthly savings, boosts profits and cash flow and enables repayment of loans and other financial obligations.

- My 4-step "bonding-with-the-team" formula for building STRONG working "bonds" with any team... that facilitates working and learning - VITAL to achieving ANY goal.

- Closely-kept negotiation secrets contractors don't want you to know. (How to use them to get the best deals reserved only for savvy buyers and best customers)

### Employment History

- GUINNESS-DIAGEO WEST AFRICA HUB – *Acting Procurement Category Manager* – Douala, Cameroon (July 2006 – April 2009)

- GUINNESS-DIAGEO WEST AFRICA HUB – *Graduate Management Trainee (on 18 months Companywide Rotation – Human Resources, Sales, Supply-Purchasing)* – Douala, Cameroon (January 2005 – June 2006)

- GUINNESS-DIAGEO WEST AFRICA HUB – *Raw Materials Storekeeper & Acting Warehouse Coordinator* – Douala, Cameroon (April 2004 – December 2005)

### Professional Training & Education

- 1 Week Training Workshop – Theme: Sourcing & Supplier Management Strategy Development and Implementation – Accra, Ghana (2008)

- Earned SPSM (Senior Professional in Supply Management) Certification – Next Level Purchasing, Inc – Pennsylvania, USA (2007 - 2008)

- Masters Degree – Industrial Engineering – ENSP, Yaoundé, Cameroon (1998 – 2003).

## The Interview-getting Résumé – Why It FORCES A Hiring Manager To Call You For An Interview

You can download a sample of it by following these steps:

1. Logon to http://jobgettingformula.com/members/signup.php by entering your first name, last name, email and password. Make sure the "Terms and Conditions" box is checked.

2. Click on "Submit".

3. Once you're logged in, click on "My Tools And Samples"

4. Click on, and download, the documents named:

   o *TheInterview-gettingRésumé-PotterExpressCo.pdf* (in Pdf format), and

   o *TheInterview-gettingRésumé-PotterExpressCo.doc* (in MS Word format)

The interview-getting résumé is simply a condensed form of the 3MM.

It clearly combines the following 4 Rules of Influence in its basic structure (but also embodies some of the other rules of influence in its content):

1. **Social Proof** in the form of Testimonials, Recommendations, Recognition Certificates, Awards, Trophies, Quotes, etc

2. **Authority** in the form of Certifications, MBAs, PhDs, JDs, Logos of prestigious companies and recognized institutions, images of recognized brands and/or products, etc.

3. **Liking - Personal Story of Achievements** in the form of Results Achieved (Selected Accomplishments), Skills Developed (Special Skills), Employers worked for (Employment History), Professional Training and Education, and others (as necessary).

4. **Special Skills written with Fascination Formulas.** Special Skills, expressed in the form of results-oriented, curiosity-boosting fascinations. This one element – alone – separates the interview-getting résumé from ALL the "mediocre" résumés existing out there. It is this one element that most forces the prospective hiring manager to call you for an interview.

Let's take a detailed look at each of its different parts and see why the interview-getting résumé is so powerful in "pushing" the hiring manager, or hiring decision maker, to call you for an interview:

1. **It's different.** It's not like an ordinary résumé, and so, that alone enables it to stand out from the crowd.

2. **It's intentionally designed as a 1-page document.** This is to ensure that all the fluffy irrelevant stuff is taken out, and only the optimally-compressed, high-impact, curiosity-boosting items are left on it. The reason for that is simply because the ONLY goal of the interview-getting résumé is to make your phone ring for an interview. Another reason for this is that, in this busy world of today, hiring managers and hiring decision makers want relevant, precise and brief information that helps them make decisions easily and quickly.

3. **It has an "Objective Summary" section** that is highly targeted, based on thorough gold-digging research about the employer's problems. It acts like an attention-grabbing headline that smacks down on the hiring manager's emotional hot buttons and informs him/her, in a specific way, of what you can achieve for them.

   **Note:** The objective summary statement of this sample interview-getting résumé is a little tweak of paragraph 52 of my 3MM. This is because that paragraph offers a direct solution to the 3 mistakes and the hiring manager's key problems. You can do the same with your 3MM and interview-getting résumé, since those are the first two documents you will be sending to your prospective hiring manager – for unadvertised positions. For advertised positions, you'll send the interview-getting résumé and interview-getting cover letter instead.

4. **It has a "Selected Accomplishments" section**. This section helps you select, summarize or sum up some of your most outstanding accomplishments into 1 to 3 powerful statements that come after, and reinforce your objective summary statement.

It condenses all what you would have written on 5 pages of résumé into high-impact, highly-targeted, carefully-selected, eye-grabbing accomplishment statements, which are related to the prospective hiring manager's problems, discovered through your gold-digging research.

They are the same as the "Results Achieved" portion of the rapport-building story section of your 3MM.

For a bonus course on how to write interest-multiplier, interview-getting accomplishment statements, go to:

http://jobgettingformula.com/members/signup.php.

Enter your name, email and password. Then, click on "My Tools And Samples" tab and download the documents named:

• *HowToWriteInterest-MultiplierInterview-gettingAccomplishments*

• *ConvertingTasksAndProjectsToAccomplishmentsExample*

5. **It has a "Special Skills" Section.** This section helps you describe 3 to 5 highly-valued skills that the employer is looking for. Make sure the special skills match your selected accomplishments, and that they are written in fascination formula style.

**Note**: These are the same "Special skills" or "Skills Developed", as mentioned in the rapport-building story section of your 3MM.

6. **It has a column where images can be placed.** Images "speak" a thousand times more emotionally than words. Another key aspect is that most logos of great companies, great training institutions, universities and great brands carry authority,

prestige and reputation that have been built over the years, and some of which can "rub off" on you and increase your perceived value when you use them on your résumé. They activate the powerful influence weapon of authority as described previously.

Make sure you use logos of organizations you've worked for or done business with – in any way, e.g. customers, training institutions, schools attended, current and former employers, etc.

But make sure they carry weight, relevance and importance in the eyes of the prospective hiring manager. It may be the logo of their major competitors or some customer they highly seek to have as part of their portfolio of big clients. It may be a business school they respect so much that they like to hire people from there, etc.

Use images of special awards, certificates of recognition, certifications in your industry, PhDs, MBAs, JDs, trophies, key products you helped launch or develop, and any image that would explain something of relevance in promoting your value.

Remember: treat your résumé like a marketing brochure. In marketing, everything makes a difference in separating you from the crowd.

7. **You can include testimonials and recommendations** in the column among the images.

Testimonials or recommendations are powerful third-party endorsements of your capabilities and they increase your credibility. They activate the influence weapon of social proof as we saw previously in the 3MM section.

Include testimonials, recommendations and praises of colleagues, clients, bosses, etc. Include anything that has been said of you anywhere, in LinkedIn, in emails, on certificates of recognition, etc.

Make sure you have proof and have sought out the permission or agreement of the person who did the recommendation for you before using it, as the employer might want to call to verify.

8. **The Employment History section**. This Section simply lists down in a chronological manner the different organizations you've worked for in the past. In order to create space, the items of the bulleted list are limited to the *name of the organization, position held, location, start* and *end dates*.

9. **Professional Training and Education section**. These sections simply offer you the opportunity to mention your academic and professional qualifications in the order you deem most relevant.

10. **Other sections**. You can also add or modify the names of one or more sections as you think would be more appropriate to sell yourself better to the employer. For example, you can include a "Professional Affiliations" section, "Hobbies" section, or "Miscellaneous" section.

# Why Putting Your Résumé Online Is A Great Idea

I recommend that you create an online version of your résumé for each employer you target, using https://www.visualcv.com. This way, you can attach the link to it at the end of your 3MM or cover letter, just as I did in my 3MM.

An online visual CV offers you the possibility to showcase yourself, your skills, qualifications and experience a thousand times more than an ordinary résumé on paper.

You can post pictures of projects you've been involved in, such as presentations you offered, seminars you attended, images and links of articles you wrote or commented on, images of community and company projects you contributed to, etc.

You may also use it as an easy reference when contacting hiring managers, as we'll see in the next Step.

It's easy to create a visual CV once you have created your original interview-getting résumé. You simply follow the easy instructions on the site and "copy and paste" from your original résumé. You'll also need to have all your images set in a folder in your computer to attach to your visual CV.

Here's the link to mine, for example: http://www.visualcv.com/slyn

# The Interview-getting Cover Letter™ (Sample)

1. Subject: **Help You MAXIMIZE Your Profits and Cash Flow... In A Way That Will Not Only Enable You Meet Up With Your Monthly Loan Repayment, BUT Help You WIN Your Banker's FULL Confidence.**

2. From: **Sly N,**

3. May 19, 2009.

4. Dear Mr. Smith,

5. Has your Company just won a new transportation contract that requires new trucks to deliver? Have you acquired new trucks with the help of a bank loan to deliver great quality transportation services to your Client? Are you afraid that, because the lucrative nature of this contract is challenged by the large number of new trucks to effectively manage, you might not have enough cash flow at the end of the month to pay back the loan?

   If you answer yes to these questions, then I have a solution that can help you.

   And that's why I think you should invite me for a meeting so that we can discuss my *unique* abilities and intended plan of action for Potter Express Co.

6. Here are a few of the Results I have achieved before and can achieve again for you:

   - **Negotiated within budget, a $5.5 million** Road Transportation Services project, by re-selecting competent Road Transportation Contractors, negotiating down prices, and establishing a 3-year contract (October 2008 – April 2009, Guinness-Diageo West Africa Hub ).

   - **Saved over $250,000** by developing and implementing savings and cost avoidance strategies on major purchase categories such as Logistics and Distribution Services, Machine Spare parts, Site Construction & Engineering Services (including CCTV), Cleaning, and General Support Services (July 2007 – April 2009, Guinness-Diageo West Africa Hub).

7. Here are the special skills I have developed that I can directly put to work for you:

   - How to "lock in" negotiated pricing, service delivery specifications, and warranties that FORCE a contractor to deliver best price, service and quality, EVERY MONTH.

   - How to avoid poor contractor service that causes truck breakdowns and financial penalties from customer - making it unlikely to meet up with monthly loan payments.

   - Certified contract-writing techniques to protect your Company from risks – like being "legally committed" to a poor performing, high-cost contractor for years. (causing loss of profits and cash flow and failures to meet up with loan repayments)

   - A "Systematic Method" for identifying, analyzing and executing cost avoidance and savings opportunities that automatically maximizes total monthly savings, boosts profits and cash flow and enables repayment of loans and other financial obligations.

   - My 4-step "bonding-with-the-team" formula for building STRONG working "bonds" with any team... that facilitates working and learning - VITAL to achieving ANY goal.

   - Closely-kept negotiation secrets contractors don't want you to know. (How to use them to get the best deals reserved only for savvy buyers and best customers)

- And much, much, more.

8. Let me know how I can start offering my help to you and your business, so that you will not only be able to satisfy your customer and boost your profits & cash flow, but you'll also be able to secure payment of your loan and become the type of customer your banker always like to do business with.

9. If you have any questions or would like us to discuss this further, please contact me.

   Sincerely,

10. Sly N

11. P.S: Again… if you really want to reduce your maintenance costs and increase your profits and cash flow…in a way that would allow you meet up with your monthly loan repayments and avoid losing the great confidence your banker has in you, then now is the time to act, especially now that I am available and ready to help. Simply call me at: 1 641 980 5516 or email me at Slyn2012@gmail.com.

12. For more information about me visit: http://www.visualcv.com/slyn

# 12 Parts That Make The Interview-getting Cover Letter A Sharp-shooting, Powerfully-persuasive Sales-letter.

Before we dive into the 12 parts of the interview-getting cover letter, let me re-emphasize what it really is.

The Merriam-Webster dictionary defines the word sharp-shooting as: 1. shooting with great precision. 2. Accurate and usually unexpected attack.

So, if your cover letter can combine the 3 ingredients of: 1. shooting with great precision. 2. Accurate and usually "unexpected attack." 3. Powerful persuasion…

…then you get the *exact power* you need to make a hiring manager call you for an interview.

This is really what your interview-getting cover letter can and must do.

You can download samples of them from the Job-getting Formula tools page at: http://jobgettingformula.com/members/signup.php.

Simply enter your name, email and password. Then, click on "My Tools And Samples" tab and download them. They are titled:

- *Interview-gettingCoverLetter-PotterExpressCo.V1*

- *Interview-gettingCoverLetter-PotterExpressCo.V2*

- *Interview-gettingCoverLetter-PotterExpressCo.V3*

- *Interview-gettingCoverLetter-PotterExpressCo.V4*

- *Interview-gettingCoverLetter-PotterExpressCo.V5*

And now, let's jump into the details:

1. **Attention-grabbing Headline.** Use the fascination formulas and write an eye-popping subject line, in bold letters, that touches on all the major emotional hot-buttons of the prospective hiring manager. This will grab your prospects attention like a magnet.

   ALWAYS START WITH THE HEADLINE!!! DON'T be tempted to follow traditional letter-writing here. This is about standing out from the crowd and getting your message across in a compelling way. It's not about boring, traditional letter-writing etiquettes. It's all about real and serious business.

   See examples of the 5 different headline formula examples you can choose from – corresponding to the 5 different cover letter versions you downloaded.

2. **From "Senders Name".** Clearly write your name, as the name of the sender.

3. **Date.** Clearly write the date you intend to mail the letter to your prospect.

4. **Salutation.** Address the person designated as the hiring manager or hiring decision maker by his/her real name. This makes it personal and builds rapport.

E.g: Dear Mr. John or Dear Mrs Elizabeth.

Do whatever it takes to have their exact names.

Your salutation is just like meeting and greeting the hiring manager or hiring decision maker in person. Remember you are doing speak-writing. So imagine that you met the hiring manager in person – would you say, "Dear Mr./Mrs. 'Whomever It May Concern'?" It would be icky if you did that in person, right? So why would you do it in your cover letter if you knew it would break rapport?

5. **Captivating Opening Paragraphs**.

The opening paragraphs of your letter must begin with a few captivating phrases that INSTANTLY create rapport with the hiring manager and commit them to reading the rest of your letter.

You can accomplish this by following one of the three options below:


**Option 1**:

**First**, use the same headline as your interview-getting résumé for your subject line.

**Second**, use the influence weapon of commitment and consistency, just like in the 3MM, by asking questions that you know the prospect must answer "Yes" to. These questions are based on the fears, frustrations, challenges and goals of the hiring manager, as found out through your gold-digging research.

**Third**, use the phrase, *"If you answer yes to these questions, then I have a solution that can help you."*

**Fourth**, use the phrase *"That's why I think we should meet so that we can discuss…"*

**Example** – the cover letter sample named:

*Interview-gettingCoverLetter-PotterExpressCo.V1*

**Option 2**:

**First,** use the same headline as your 3MM report for your subject line.

**Second**, use the same commitment and consistency questions as in option 1 to invoke "yes" answers.

**Third**, use the phrase, *"If you answer yes to these questions, then you are probably making one or more of these 3 mistakes:"*

**Fourth**, state the 3 dangerous mistakes the prospect is making that are aggravating the problem.

**Fifth**, use the phrase *"That's why I think we should meet so that we can discuss..."*

**Example** – the cover letter sample named:

*Interview-gettingCoverLetter-PotterExpressCo.V2*


**Option 3**:

**First**, use one of the 3 BIG mistakes in the subject line. Link the mistake directly to the major emotional hot buttons of the prospect. Use the fascination formula *Why [Result Happens/Problem Happens]* followed by the phrase *"...And What To Do About It"*.

**Second**, clearly address (or describe in detail) the chosen mistake. Speak-write in "what" and "why" style about the mistake and amplify the moving-away-from and moving-towards motivators.

**Third**, use the phrase *"That's why I think we should meet so that we can discuss..."*

**Examples** – the 3 cover letter samples corresponding to each of the 3 mistakes in my 3MM, taken one at a time:

*Interview-gettingCoverLetter-PotterExpressCo.V3.*

*Interview-gettingCoverLetter-PotterExpressCo.V4*

*Interview-gettingCoverLetter-PotterExpressCo.V5*

6. **Results - "Here are a few of the Results I have achieved before and can achieve again for you"** :

   This is simply where you share the results you've achieved in the past, that are relevant or related to the prospects problems or similar to the results they want.

   These are basically the same selected accomplishments you mentioned in your résumé and 3MM.

7. **Skills - "Here are the special skills I have developed that I can directly put to work for you":**

   This is where you put your fascinations to work for you like crazy. In copywriting parlance, we call these your "marketing bullets."

   The role of these "mouth-wetting" bullet points is to arouse the prospect's curiosity to a point where they are compelled to call you for an interview.

8. The **Call to Action**.

   This is where you state clearly what you want your prospect to do. It's your offer to help as well as the benefits and payoff the prospect will get if they hire you.

9. **Ask for questions.** *"If you have any questions or would like us to discuss this further, please contact me."*

   It also helps to "push" the prospect to action.

10. **Your Signature**: It's simply writing your name after the word "Sincerely". Easy, huh?

11. The **P.S.** or **Postscript** – the most read part of every letter.

    I know you must have seen this in most letters… but what, in your opinion, is the role of the P.S.?

Usually, when somebody picks up a letter, there's a high tendency to look below to see the person who wrote it and judge from their signature.

And the P.S. is located, as you know, just below the signature or name of the person who wrote the letter. That causes the reader to almost always read it, in every letter.

Masters of sales and advertising copywriting have known this secret for nearly a century. Now I am sharing it with you, and so… it's your time to start using it to your favor with your cover letters.

The P.S. may serve as a conclusion and summary of the key points to drive home with the letter. It often capitalizes on the one major idea you want the reader to stay with or the one action you want them to take.

In this case, that one action is to call you for an interview. So you simply restate another call to action asking the hiring manager to contact you if he/she is really serious about solving their problem.

12. **A link to your visual CV**. This will enable the prospect to see more of the "cool" things (and other portfolios) about you that can't fit into your paper résumé, cover letter or 3MM.

The visual CV offers much room for that. But make sure what you put there is relevant to your prospect's problems, in a way that would build credibility rather than destroy it.

**Note**: Create separate résumés, cover letters, 3MM and visual CVs for different prospective employers.

As you must have noticed, the different versions of interview-getting cover letters exploit additional rules of influence, such as Commitment and Consistency, Scarcity, Powerful Persuasion, 4 Learning Styles and Reciprocation, all of which could not be used in your interview-getting résumé.

The interview-getting cover letter, together with your interview-getting résumé, will complement each other, in terms of coverage of the majority, but not all, of the 13 rules of influence used in the 3MM. This is because the interview-getting cover letter is a shortened version of your 3MM.

## How To Use The 5 Different Versions Of The Interview-getting Cover Letters

Use the first one as the first you send to the hiring manager, and the four others as follow-ups, at regular intervals, e.g. weekly or bi-weekly, until you are called for an interview.

If you started by sending a 3MM, which is what is recommended for all unadvertised positions, then use all 5 of the cover letters as follow-ups at regular intervals.

NEVER send a 3MM and a cover letter together. It's either the 3MM and your résumé or your cover letter and résumé. This is because the interview-getting cover letter is designed as a short form of your 3MM.

The reason we follow up is that we may never know what happened to the letter along the way. Maybe, it was never opened by the hiring manager. Or it was read in a hasty mood or they were interrupted while reading it. Or they are still waiting and deliberating with their superiors before taking action. Or they are still procrastinating on whether to call you or not. Or the letter simply did not touch their true issues and emotional hot buttons.

By following up, you can fine-tune your research further, or tweak your letter a bit. Both will drastically improve your results.

Statistics have shown that often people take some time before making a complex buying decision. In the same way, they may take some time to make a hiring decision, which is a sort of complex buying decision.

So keep bombarding them with your cover letter "missiles" at regular intervals. If after the fifth attempt, you have no response, they may simply not be ready to hire anybody at the moment. Move on to the next company on your list. That's why I asked you to choose 10 companies and experiment with 1 or 2 of the least important in your list, before moving up to the favorites, as you become a pro with the job-getting formula skills.

If it was an open position you applied for and even after several follow-ups you were not called for an interview, then probably you simply did not do your research well to find out the true emotional hot buttons of your prospect.

In a rare case where you *really* think you've done all your best with using the interview-getting cover letters and other techniques, simply describe what you did by sending me a question at:

sylvester@jobgettingformula.com

And I will support you in finding a solution to your problem.

But, right now, I think you've got the best I can offer you in terms of cutting edge job-getting techniques and strategies (within the limits set for this book). The only thing you have to do is to put them correctly to work. You can also subscribe to my free supplementary training videos at:

www.JobgettingFormula.com

Thanks for reading this far. And now, let's move on to the next Step of the Job-getting Formula…

# The Job getting Formula

## STEP 4

## Can You CONTACT The Employer And Let Them Know You Can Deliver Results, Better Than Any Other Candidate? (Here's The Mature & Skillful Way)

I know if you are from the "popular school," like most people, you'd be surprised by simply hearing that hiring managers really want people to contact them and offer to help solve a particular problem they are facing.

What most people would say is that the last thing a hiring manager would want you to contact them for is to ask them for a job... let alone a high-paying job. And they are right.

Read my lips. I said, *"offer to help solve a particular problem."* I didn't say they want us to contact them and ask for a job.

No hiring manager wants to be embarrassed by someone asking for a job. You know for sure that they don't run charity or socialist organizations where there is a job for everybody who simply asks for it.

But here's what they want:

They want someone who knows the problems they are trying to solve and are offering to help find a solution.

These are two completely different approaches. In the first case, someone is asking for a job or a pay check. In the second case, someone is offering to help – though at the end they'll be paid for their services. You see what I mean?

EVERYBODY, at some time, has a preoccupying problem to solve. It may be a problem at work or a personal one. But everybody always wants a solution to their problem. And they'd be happy to find someone to show up and say, "I can help."

So, as you can see, the most important thing for you to know is: what big problem is my prospective hiring manager trying to solve at work? What goal are they trying to achieve? Do they have an appropriate solution for it? Or are they messing things up?

Can you find out exactly what they need, do some research, adapt your skills, take on some new projects in the domain in which they are having a problem, get some results, and offer to help?

Once you know what they want, and you've found a solution to offer, it becomes very easy to simply walk up to them and say: *"Hey, do you have such and such problem? Are you making these mistakes? See, I have done this before, and I know how to help solve the problem. I have developed the following skills that are guaranteed to get you results. Would you like me to join your team and work out the solution for you?"*

This is what every hiring manager expects you to do. You can contact them in this way without any problem. This is what I mean when I say that the number-4 BIG question every hiring manager is asking is: *"Can you contact me and let me know you can deliver results, better than any other candidate?"*

So, if you've been following me up to this point, let's review what you've done, or are supposed to have done so far.

You've determined the 10 companies you want to work for. You've used the gold-digging and situational assessment questions to figure out exactly what problems the hiring manager is pre-occupied with. You've used "possibility thinking" to design a solution to their problem. You've tested some critical elements of the solution and you know the solution works. You've come up with what you can qualify as 3 big mistakes the hiring manager and their team are making. You've developed your 3 mistakes marketing around those mistakes, as well as your interview-getting résumé and 5 versions of interview-getting cover letters. And now, you're set to go meet the hiring manager and give them your 3MM and Interview-getting résumé.

So, what else can stop you at this point?

Well, this is what I am sure of: probably the "monster" called the "Fear of Rejection" is going to stop you, as it does with most people.

You see, most people often rely on someone to introduce them to someone else they have never met before... not really because it is more polite that way, as they say. But because... they are afraid of rejection and would like to use the other person as a "rejection shield." I know this because I have been guilty of this approach myself.

But here's what I found: It's easier to manage your success by walking up to people and introducing yourself and then building a relationship from there than it is to wait for somebody else to do it for you.

Moreover, it builds a stronger relationship, because the other person quickly recognizes the interest you have in them and the courage you've mustered to come across and talk to them.

Many people, because they are afraid of rejection, have found an easier way. They post hundreds of résumés to various HR departments, online job boards, and recruiting agencies and "pray" for the hiring manager to get it and then call them.

While successful people also pray, they have found that God helps those who help themselves. They take control and responsibility for their actions. They focus on that which they can control. And they know that taking control means relying less on the actions of others, especially if you know you won't be compensating them in any way for their help.

Those who succeed find out about the people they would like to meet, the places they go to, and the activities they like. And they do everything to go meet them there and talk to them face-to-face.

If they know that the CEO they want to meet plays golf in the famous golf club down town, they start spending their weekends going to watch him/her play. They observe carefully for the right moment to walk over to them and deliver their message of relief.

In the process, they master and conquer the fear of rejection.

Today, in a highly connected world, you might not even need to meet your prospect physically. You can meet them online – on social media sites like Facebook, LinkedIn, Myspace, etc.

But before I show you how to use all of these different means to contact your prospective hiring manager, let me tell you more about…

## The "Mythic Monster" *Called* "Fear Of Rejection" – Its Origins And Why It Can STOP You And Destroy All Your Dreams Of Getting A High-paying Job – And What To Do About It

From my own personal experience and from coaching and talking to job seekers, one of the things that hold most people back from talking DIRECTLY to hiring managers, hiring decision makers and other people is that they don't want to come out as being an unwanted "pest," because they fear that this may lead to them being rejected.

But unfortunately enough, this type of mindset is a "loser" and is one that doesn't get results or achieve worthy goals… such as that of getting a high-paying job.

Getting a high-paying job with a success-sized salary will require you to interact with people, and in particular, informants and hiring managers, who might be top level managers, heads of departments or other hiring decision makers.

To be able to do this, you MUST change the way you THINK about the fear of rejection, which pops up during the process of *thinking of contacting, actually contacting* and *interacting* with people you've not met before.

I know from personal experience that the PAIN of the fear of rejection, combined with the PAIN of not being able to control it... combined with the PAIN of it not making ANY sense at all... can really affect a person's self image and self esteem.

The reason I want to spend some time going over the FEAR aspect of approaching hiring managers and informants... and taking time to not only explain how and why it's happening and where it comes from, but also how to get PAST it... is because… if you don't get it and then get past it... it can literally CONTROL YOUR LIFE, and lock you up in the prison of mediocrity FOREVER.

Contacting people is like selling. And I am not talking about the sleazy type of salespeople, who try to force people to buy what they don't want. Real, honest, high-integrity selling… is walking up to people you've never met before, but who have a problem and need a solution, and telling them how you can be of help to them.

But when it comes to selling, most people have a mindset that PREVENTS them from becoming a real salesperson, at least the type of salesperson whose one and most important job is to SELL his/her skills and personal services, in the form of a high-paying job, to hiring managers and hiring decision makers, who *desperately* need their service.

We have to change the way we consider rejection, simply because it is part of the human interactive process and we MUST know how to handle it and deal with it.

While at first sight, it may seem as if it is an issue out of our control… from years of studying the human mind and its influence on human interactions and success, I can tell you this:

The feeling of rejection is a MYTH that we carry in our heads based on the level of our self image, self esteem and self confidence – all three of which are part of that part of us called the *ego*.

The fact is that most people DO feel an intense, irrational, uncontrollable FEAR when they even THINK about approaching a stranger. Not to talk of a hiring manager, for that matter.

So, why do we feel like we're risking DEATH when we think of approaching a hiring manager we don't know, for the first time?

There are many reasons to that. But here are 3 major ones:

### 1. We Don't Want To Be Considered An Unwanted "Pest"

We know for sure that hiring managers may consider us as one of the crowd of people who often call them and embarrass them, saying: "I need a job" or "I want to apply for a job."

And guess what? Unfortunately, that's what every hiring manager expects. They know that 9 out of 10 people who call them or meet them often do so for selfish reasons.

However, there is a direct link between the fear of rejection from a hiring manager AND not knowing the problem a hiring manager really wants to solve – for which they'll happily welcome any proposal of a solution.

And if we've not properly done our gold-digging research to know exactly what the hiring manager wants, we'll lack the confidence to move up to the hiring manager and talk to them – simply because we'll be a little skeptical about our offer. We know it will end up sounding like we're begging for a job.

But if you take your time and dig into what the hiring manger really wants, then you'll automatically move from being an "unwanted pest" to being an "invited guest."

Let me share a little story with you that will make you NEVER to fear rejection again.

While jogging one Saturday morning, I ended up at a Barnes & Noble bookshop to check out new arrivals of books. And I saw this little great book titled *The Millionaire Messenger*. It happened to have been written by one of my teachers, Brendon Burchard. I decided to buy the book, but didn't have enough cash on me. I was down by 2 dollars. I also didn't have any credit card on me since I was jogging.

So, the natural thing for me to have done was to go back home and come back some other day to get the book. On a second thought, I said to myself: why not beg for the 2 dollars from the lady cashier? Why go back home without the book only because of 2 dollars – and only because I don't want to embarrass or bother someone?

So, I asked the lady cashier if she could help me with the 2 dollars. Greatly embarrassed, she shrugged her shoulders, saying, "Sorry I don't have any cash on me." I wasn't surprised, because I'm used to rejection. And I knew there were only two options: she either gives me the money or says she doesn't have any.

So I gave myself the challenge to raise 2 dollars by talking to anybody else who was in the bookshop. Luckily, I talked to another lady who gave me the only dollar she had as cash. Then, I talked to another who *angrily* told me she didn't have it. Next was a man who smiled and said, "Sorry, nada" (meaning "nothing", in Spanish). Then, I met this last lady who finally and happily asked me if 4 quarter dollars, in coins, would do. I said. "No problem." I gladly went back to the counter and bought the book.

I know this little 2-dollar problem may sound obvious. But there are people who'll prefer to postpone their actions for a day or more, no matter how small that action may be, for fear of making themselves and others a bit uncomfortable.

Just as I wanted to go home and come back some other day to buy that book, some people will prefer that option, simply because they are afraid to be considered an unwanted "pest." That's how many people postpone their success forever. They don't know that opportunity is ALWAYS, always, always mixed with a bit of difficulty. It has taken me almost an entire lifetime to understand this indisputable fact about opportunity.

But here are other lessons this little story teaches:

**Lesson #1**: Some people will be more embarrassed than the person asking for help, especially when you're asking for help they cannot provide. Just like the lady cashier who was embarrassed for not having two dollars to help me, so too will a hiring manager who doesn't have a job to offer you. But the bottom line is… you have nothing to lose, but much to gain, if only you ask.

In this case, I was asking for two dollars. But in your case, you may want to *help* save, sell, or protect two thousand, two hundred thousand, or two million dollars for the hiring manager and employer. Therefore, you have nothing to lose either, but rather much to gain. So too is the hiring manager.

**Lesson #2**: Some people will refuse or reject you, like the other lady and the man did to me. But again, that takes nothing from you. It only adds to your self esteem and self-confidence for having tried.

**Lesson #3**: Someone will offer you the help, so long as you keep asking. Like the other 2 ladies did to me. Again, you win. That's why I suggested you choose 10 companies, because some hiring managers will reject you, for one reason or the other. But some will accept you.

So, go out and talk to people, ask for help and ask to offer help. And to hiring managers, in particular, *only* seek ways to offer them help. You'd be glad you did.

## 2. We Want To Secure Approval By NOT "Hurting" The Hiring Manager's Feelings

Let me now share with you why our parents' "good intentions" of making us become "good people" is actually a major cause of the fear of rejection in us. I think this astonishing insight will enable you to quickly throw away your fear of rejection.

We first learned the fear of rejection and approval-seeking when we were children – when our parents made their love conditional upon our behavior.

When we did what was pleasing to them and what was considered by them as good for us, they gave us their love and approval.

When we did something they didn't like, they withdrew their love and approval…and of which, since then, we've continuously interpreted as rejection. And we've grown up to adulthood still carrying this mythic fear called rejection.

We now consider the hiring manager or hiring decision maker the same way we considered our parents, guardians and other people of any authority level… and in doing so, we try to be compliant in order NOT to hurt their feelings, and we'll rather do everything to gain their approval, even at the expense of us coming off as being immature.

## 3. We Fear The Unknown

We fear that *anything* can happen.

One of my prospects hooked up with me on Facebook, asking for help in getting a job. Then as usual, I used the gold-digging research technique to dig deep into what his real problems or obstacles were.

The following is an excerpt of our coaching conversation. For privacy reasons, I have left out his name. But the most important thing is for you to see how the fear of rejection is manifested through the fear of the unknown.

I started by asking him: *"So tell me... what's your greatest frustration when it comes to getting a job?"*

He said: *"I think... panic at the interview when there are more than 4 staff members present."*

I said: *"Ok, so you get panicked."*

He said: *"I am not that bold before so many people."*

I asked: *"What causes the panic? Or what do you think is the cause?"*

He said: *"It is innate. But it has been decreasing as I've grown older."*

I dug deep, and asked: *"If there's one thing you're afraid about in talking to people you don't know before, what is it?"*

He pointed out: *"Their characters and behavior I am unfamiliar with."* (Notice the fear of the unknown.)

I went on (trying to nail the issue), and asked: *"Ok. So what do you think can stop you from asking somebody you don't know for an interview?"*

He replied: *"If they are intimidating."*

I asked: *"Ok, so does that mean fear of rejection?"*

He answered: *"Yes, it does."*

I asked: *"Ok. Would you like to learn how to handle rejection?"*

He said: *"Yes."*

I said: *"Ok, so the first exercise I will give you to fight rejection is simple. Are you ready?"*

He said: *"Yes"*

I said: *"Ok. Make sure you go to a strange place like a supermarket or a busy street and talk to 3 people, 3 times a week - 3 people you don't know."*

He said: *"Yes"*

I hinted: *"Just say to them, for example, that 'Hey, your car, or your suit, or hairstyle or dress or etc, is nice. Would you mind if I ask you a question?' And ask them how they feel about their job. And tell them that you're doing research to find out how people feel about their jobs."*

He said: *"Ok."*

I went on to say: *"Copy this exercise and make sure you do it. It will improve your self-confidence and initiate you into a new world of achievers."*

I warned: *"And expect only 2 results. They'll talk to you or tell you they are busy. Now that you know how they'll react, GO NOW. And let me have your feedback on this small, but powerful exercise."*

He said: *"Ok, I understand."*

He went on and said: *"I will give you some results next week."*

The following week,

I asked him: *"Hi, how are you doing? What were the results of the Rejection Test?"*

He answered: *"Those people were arrogant in responding... is anything fishy about the question?"*

I said: *"Please describe me exactly what happened. Let me see how it really went. Tell me, step by step, how you went about it."*

He said: *"First, I met an Indian, who was a manager in a supermarket. He welcomed me and asked me to sit down. After introducing myself, I went on with the question. Before then, he put a smile on his face but shortly after the question he was very angry and asked me to leave the office, that somebody was waiting for him outside. I believe if I were in India, that man would have sent me behind bars. Well, I will explain the other experience later... I do not have enough time left at the cybercafé."*

I explained: *"If all you just explained to me really took place, then I'll simply say BRAVO, because the 'fear of rejection' can only be conquered through multiple rejections. You just got your first rejection. You need more... to finally discover that rejection doesn't KILL. It only builds more courage. But the most important thing is that, out of every ten experiences, you'll get 4 rejections, 3 successes, and 3 no-rejection-no-success or no 'hard feelings'. Go Ahead! Kudos!"*

So, what is the lesson to learn here? And why did I bring this conversation up?

- **The first** reason, is to show you "live" how the fear of rejection is manifested.

- **The second** is to prove to you that we grew up with this fear.

The proof is in the following lines:

I asked: *"What causes the panic? Or what do you think is the cause?"*

He said: *"It is innate. But it has been decreasing as I've grown older."*

- **The third** is to prove to you that we really fear the "unknown."

Notice the lines:

*"He welcomed me and asked me to sit down. After introducing myself, I went on with the question. Before then he put a smile on his face but shortly after the question, he was very angry and asked me to leave the office, that somebody was waiting for him outside. I believe if I were in India that man would have sent me behind bars."*

NO, NO, NO. It's NOT true that someone can get you locked up behind bars for simply talking to them. The Indian man simply said *"somebody is waiting for him out outside."* Right?

I understand. It's just fear... just a false and weird image in the mind. That's why somebody rightly said FEAR = False Evidence Appearing Real.

I heard once that something like 98% of the things that people fear and worry about never come true. I've found this to be true in my own life, as well.

- **The fourth** reason is that it's a game of winning and losing. That's why I told him:

  *"...out of every ten experiences, you'll get 4 rejections, 3 successes, and 3 no-rejection-no-success or no hard feelings."*

- **The fifth and final** reason is to prove that rejection does NOT KILL. It only makes you stronger. (Want Proof? The guy who was rejected is still alive and doing very well with his career.)

## Fear Is Good In Some Ways

Apart from the negative aspects of fear, which stop us from achieving our goals, fear is quite a vital emotion. It is part of our genetic "makeup." It was given to us by the Creator to prepare us for flight or escape when faced with real physical danger, like when an animal tries to attack us.

When you feel fear in response to real physical danger, you'll notice that some AMAZING things happen. Your eyes open up wider so you can see better, adrenaline pumps into your body, your heart beats fast to deliver blood to your muscles, and all kinds of other wondrous processes are triggered to prepare you for immediate flight. Fear is a life-saving emotion.

The PROBLEM is when we experience fear at times when there is NO real *physical danger* - when it's just adult-to-adult interaction - like when we want to pick up the phone to call a prospective hiring manager and nail down a high-paying job opportunity.

Have you heard of "Call Reluctance?" Amazing!

Imagine how the fear of rejection can FREEZE and IMMOBILIZE you at critical moments... like when making a 3-minute, single phone call can earn you a high-paying job and change your life, in the best case... or simply leave you with an increased and healthy self-confidence for having tried, in the worst case.

But here's where it gets even more interesting and counter-intuitive. By counter-intuitive, I mean that it's something you've probably never thought of... in the sense that, actually...

## Rejection Is A Form Of Test You Go Through In The Course Of Being Hired

Many people would use rejection, consciously or unconsciously, to get you off their backs when you are requesting something.

But that's not all.

The very busy people at the top of the career hierarchy, such as hiring managers and hiring decision makers...do use rejection even more... to see whether you are "ripe" and mature enough for the types of claims you make.

You bet... If you want to get a high-paying job, the claims you make have to be big. And you'll be tested for both your savvy and your maturity. Most hiring managers will use rejection as a test of your maturity.

This is because, as you may know, the most difficult part of every job is dealing with people from different backgrounds and mentalities...

and therefore, a lot of rejection to handle. That's mostly what gets many people stressed out at their jobs.

This form of Rejection-testing would generally reveal to whoever is the "tester," some great insight about the entire personality of the person who is being tested – in this case, you.

What is weird with this whole "rejection test" thing is that most often, you won't even know you are being tested. Amazingly also, the tester usually does the testing most of the time unconsciously while interacting with you – it's like a "program" in our subconscious mind.

But in the process, they gather impressions about you that tell them a TON about the type of person you are. And this progressively shapes their decision about whether to hire you or not.

That means, you certainly must pass the rejection test before you qualify for the high-paying job you want.

I mean, let's look at it this way:

Imagine you saying, in your résumé and cover letter, that you have great interpersonal skills… when you can't prove it in these types of interpersonal interactions with people such as the hiring manager. That alone will quickly enable the hiring manager to exclude you, as rapidly as possible.

## The Rejection-proof Formula (or How To Conquer The Fear of Rejection)

Let me now show you a step-by-step formula to defeat rejection FOREVER.

I am doing this because I know if you still have any trace of fear of rejection in your mind, and allow it to drive your decisions and choices, then it will surely lower your self-image. And it'll negatively affect your tone of voice, your body language, and how you communicate… even in the words you use in your 3MM, cover letter and résumé. All these documents are just a representation of your inner state of mind.

Remember, with these documents, you're trying to do influential speak-writing, which is just like talking face-to-face to the hiring manager, but in print form.

If you fear rejection, it will lower your self-esteem and will make you come across as timid with your claims and with your offer – both written and spoken.

And the bad part is that any hiring manager will notice it. People in general and hiring managers in particular know that anyone who's mature enough, who's sure of what he/she knows and can do, doesn't need approval and is not afraid of rejection.

Now that we know what the fear of rejection is all about, let me give you a mental technique to conquer it forever.

I first learned this technique from the legendary Anthony Robbins, in his book *Unlimited Power – The Way To Peak Personal Achievement* And since then, I have been "mixing" it with what I have been told repeatedly by my other teacher, Bob Proctor. And I have been practicing it all the time, whenever I have to meet somebody new for the first time – such as prospective clients in my consulting business, people I need special favors from, etc. It works pretty well.

The technique is based on the fact that we humans have a mental image of all the things we've encountered and those that we imagine encountering.

To keep it simple, we think in pictures. Whenever we think of doing something, the image of that thing flashes in the "screen" of our mind. It then creates a feeling – positive or negative, that will move us towards positive or negative action.

In other words, our thinking influences our feelings which influence our behavior or actions.

Now, let's apply this to what we know about the fear of rejection. Remember, when we have fear of something, it's essentially because of the negative image of that thing in our mind.

When we think of approaching and talking to somebody who's strange to us, we form a mental image of that person in our mind as being rude, ruthless, intimidating and unwelcoming to us. This makes us have the *feeling* or emotion of fear. And it makes us feel less motivated to talk to that person.

This is then reflected in the tone of our voice, our body language (e.g. fallen shoulders, if we are greeting the person physically), and the choice of words we use (we tend to use 1-dollar words instead of 100-dollar words.)

But from what we've learned so far, we've seen that there are three possible outcomes from any interaction with a stranger:

- Outcome #1: They may listen to what you say and comply with you.

- Outcome #2: They may reject you.

- Outcome #3: They may just be somewhere around the middle – no hard feelings, just a "good to know you" type of response.

So what do we do?

We simply play three separate "movies" in our mind of the 3 possibilities, before approaching the hiring manager.

Here are the steps to follow:

1. Close your eyes.

2. Visualize the negative possibility (Outcome #2). Then, destroy the movie's quality, by simply taking away the colors of the images: the brightness, the contrast, and do everything that will make the movie blurred and non-existent, like zooming away from it and making it tiny like a dot. Then, you discard it from your mind. (I like to put it on an explosive, in my visualization, and explode it.)

3.  Focus on the positive possibilities: Outcome #1 and #3. Magnify and improve on the quality of the image. Zoom in and see the elements bigger and clearer. Add more colors, brightness and contrast. Visualize the hiring manager smiling, nodding their head with acceptance or saying something like, *"Sure I understand..."* Then, feel excited and confident about it. This will make you feel fired up and ready to go talk to them.

4.  Repeat these steps a couple of times, until you're completely fired up, before meeting or talking to the hiring manager or decision maker.

    **Note**: This process can be done instantly before approaching the hiring manager or any other unfamiliar person you want to talk to, and it will instantly "reset" your emotions and get you ready. This is the Rejection-proof formula. It's super-effective. Just make sure you follow the steps.

# How To Contact A Hiring Manager Or Hiring Decision Maker *Directly* On The Phone And Send Them Your 3MM & Interview-getting Résumé

Search for the phone number of the person running the department (who is probably the hiring manager or hiring decision maker) and contact them directly.

Use your network to get their phone number. Once you get their phone number, call the person and introduce yourself saying the following:

*"My name is_____. I've been researching the problems facing your company and your department in particular. And I have discovered a strategy (or technique)... that will help you [**get "emotional hot button" results or avoid "emotional hot button" problems, as found in the gold-digging research**]. Would you like me to send you the details about the strategy (or technique) and how I can help you implement it?"*

Here is an example (see underlined sentences):

*"My name is <u>Sly N</u>. I've been researching the problems facing your company and your department in particular. And I have discovered a strategy (or technique)... that will help you [<u>save up to 20 cents out of every dollar you spend on maintenance so that you can maximize your profits and cash flow, meet the monthly repayment of your bank loans and WIN the full confidence of your banker forever</u>]. Would you like me to send you the details about the strategy (or technique) and how I can help you implement it?"*

If they say yes, and they would say so most of the time, ask for their postal address and email address and send them a hard color-printed copy of your interview-getting résumé and 3MM in an envelope, personally addressed to them. Also send them PDF electronic versions of both documents in an email.

If they ask you a few questions like, "What it is you really want?," etc., just stick to this same script and keep saying...

*"I've been researching the problems facing your company and your department in particular. And I have discovered a strategy (or technique)... that will help you [**get "emotional hot button" results or avoid "emotional hot button" problems, as found in the gold-digging research**]. Would you like me to send you the details about the strategy (or technique) and how I can help you implement it?"*

One powerful psychological trigger that is playing here is the arousal of their curiosity. If they keep on asking you to tell them what it is all about or what technique you are talking about, NEVER be tempted to tell them that it is your résumé and some other document. Instead add the following variation (see underlined sentences) to the previous script. This is because it gets a powerful message across that you are somebody to take seriously.

So, no matter how many times they may insist... just keep saying...

*"<u>I am just really interested in your company and department. And so</u>, I've been researching the problems facing your company and your*

*department in particular. And I have discovered a strategy (or technique)... that will help you [get "emotional hot button" results or avoid "emotional hot button" problems, as found in the gold-digging research]. Would you like me to send you the details about the strategy (or technique) and how I can help you implement it? Even better, I can meet you to show you and hand it to you. Where and when do you want us to meet?"*

If you keep insisting and tweaking this initial script, thereby handling every test of rejection the person tries to throw at you, at one point, they'll either give you a place and time to meet or ask you to send it to them.

If they give you an appointment in person, then get ready to go there, well dressed and well prepared, to hand them your interview-getting résumé and 3MM. And also be prepared for an unexpected interview. (In *Step 5* of this book, I will show you how to prepare and ace in-person interviews.)

If they ask you to send it, send it by FedEx or any express mail delivery service. Then make sure you call them a few hours after it is delivered to find out if they got it. This step is very important. It makes them know that you are serious and it also helps you know if they got it.

The interesting part with this type of behavior is that it completely sets you apart from the masses of job seekers who spend their time begging for jobs. You'll come across more like an expert, a consultant or somebody confident in their abilities... and this is the *golden trait* employers are looking for in great candidates for high-paying jobs.

I have personally used this technique to get consulting jobs from most of my clients and it works very well. Try it and your life will never be the same again, in terms of the enormous gains in self esteem and self-confidence you'll get. You'll discover the power of curiosity and control over a conversation as some of the strongest forces in marketing and sales. Most people have never experienced the type of great feeling I am talking about here.

You may ask, are they using rejection to test only my interpersonal skill?

The answer is NO.

They consciously or subconsciously test a wide range of different skills, such as: your salesmanship, persuasiveness, ability to control a conversation, persistence, ability to get someone's attention, your negotiation skills, creativeness, ability to take initiative, personal poise (a.k.a maturity, stability and self-control), ability to clearly articulate verbally, etc.

Let's see how the hiring manager can possibly test you in the last conversation.

Let's assume that, despite trying to be tough, the hiring manager insists that you tell him/her directly what your technique is all about. And let's say you succumbed to the pressure and said something like… *"Well, I'd like to give you my résumé and cover letter for a job opening or any future job opening in your department."*

What do you think will be going on in the hiring manager's head at this point?

Well, they will possibly look at you as one among the thousands of job seekers who are desperately looking for a paycheck without necessarily having any valuable contribution to offer in return.

This is because there are certain things hiring managers look for in great candidates for a job (the 'A' players)… such as: drive and passion to deliver results as well as commitment to problem solving, service and excellence.

But most importantly, hiring managers know that 'A' players are more interested in first demonstrating their value and work skills to an employer, in any way they can, than they are interested in asking for a job over the phone.

And clearly, as you can see, all these things are lacking in your words when you simply say you want to give them your application for a job. That is like saying that you don't want to allow them time to discover you before eliminating you – rather, you make it so easy for them to file you in the ranks of ordinary job seekers or "paycheck mongers," right from the start.

Now, what do you think would be the hiring manager's response?

Well, I guess they'll give you an answer like... *"We're not hiring now and we don't even plan to hire any time from now."*

Or, *"Send your application to HR and they'll channel it to me later whenever there happens to be an opening."*

Well, this is not what you wanted. Right?

All they are trying to do is to "get rid of you" and move forward with their daily activities, as quickly as possible.

Now, let's assume that, despite the pressure the manager puts on you to reveal what your technique is all about, and being a tough person who wants to make the hiring manager know that you are mature and confident in your abilities, you simply stick to your script.

What do you expect the hiring manager's reaction to be?

Hmmm, I guess they'd quickly realize they've got somebody trying to sell them something, because you just touched on their "What's in it for me?" – their key problem or some of their emotional hot buttons.

And their reaction would automatically (or subconsciously) be to check out your credibility and personal motives first. But all the same, you've got their attention and that's the most important thing going for you at this point.

So, they'll probably say something like any of the following:

*"Who are you and what's your business?"* or...

*"Are you trying to sell me something?"* or...

*"How did all this research stuff of yours came about and why do you think I am the best person to talk to?"* or...

*"By the way, how did you get my phone number to contact me?"*

Or some other wacky question.

Now, what do you think is going on here?

Let me help you out.

What they are trying to do is a multitude of things:

## 1) First, they may be trying to discover whether you are AUTHENTIC.

They consciously or unconsciously want you to re-affirm what you are saying. They want you to speak out again and from there, they'll have the opportunity to listen again and "read" the tone of your voice to tell whether you seem confident about your *bold* claims or not.

**Question**: So, what's the right thing to do, to get past this?

**Here's the way forward:**

To the question about: *"How did all this research stuff of yours came about and why do you think I am the best person to talk to?,"* be calm and take your time to pause, rephrase and articulate your claims with a slight variation of the initial script and with confidence and poise.

Just be authentic and stick to your script and its slight variations, because you now have control of the conversation.

## 2) Second, they may be trying to INTIMIDATE and DISTRACT you to see if you can keep control over the conversation.

Remember, you just made a bold claim and they want to see whether you can stay consistent and keep control of the conversation you initiated. In other words, they are trying to take the lead of the conversation and testing how you'll react.

**Question**: What's the right thing to do, to get past this?

**Here's the way forward:**

You don't yield to the distraction and you don't hand over the lead of the conversation to them. It's your first and only opportunity to show them that you are a real leader. So show them – stick to your script.

To the distracting question that says, *"By the way, how did you get my phone number to contact me?"* say something like…

*"Well, you know… this is my job and once I figure out that there is so much opportunity to (save a great deal of money for a company, for example)… [or get whatever "emotional hot button" results or avoid whatever "emotional hot button" problems, as found in the gold-digging research], I take it as my responsibility to do whatever I can to get my message to the person concerned. So in the long process of my research, I found your number and since it's a long story, I thought it'd be great to reserve that for whenever we meet to discuss about the strategy (or technique) I am about to offer. Would you like me to send you the strategy (or technique)?*

3) **They may be trying to check if you are SERIOUS, if you are a *real* PROFESSIONAL or A player.**

**Question**: What's the right thing to do, to get past this?

**Here's the way forward:**

To the question of: *"Who are you and what's your business?"* or *"Are you trying to sell me something?"*…simply say something like...

*"I am a [whatever title is appropriate for the type of high-paying job you want] (e.g. Business Management Professional/Purchasing Professional/ IT Professional/ Specialist/ Consultant, etc.), and I help companies [get "emotional hot button" results or avoid "emotional hot button" problems, as found in the gold-digging research] (for example, save money, sell more, protect assets, save lives, etc)…"*

Then continue with the initial script, saying… *"I've been researching the problems facing your Company and your…"*

If, however, no matter how hard you try to convince them, they are still not interested in getting your findings and how you can help, then simply ignore them and move on to the next company in your list.

This type of behavior from them tells you why their department is having the problems it has and why there's a very high probability that they are the cause of the problems, because they are simply not open to suggestions for improvement, and I don't think that's the type of place in which you'd like to work.

## How To Contact The Hiring Manager Or Hiring Decision Maker Directly On LinkedIn

If you don't have the phone number of the hiring manager, or you've not been able to have them on phone, you can contact them directly, using LinkedIn.

1.  Go join LinkedIn.com, if you've not yet done so.

2.  After joining LinkedIn.com, which is the best place to network with other professionals, especially those working in your targeted companies, click on "Advance Search" next to the search box.

3.  Type in the search parameters. Fill the country name, company name. Under Company, between "current or past,", select "current" and click on the search button.

4.  On the search parameters column on the left, type in the first name or last name of the hiring manager you are searching for.

5.  Click on the search button at the bottom of the search parameters column.

6.  You'll be given all the search results corresponding to that first name or last name. See whether you have the full name of the person you're searching for in the short list of search results.

7. If you find them, hover your mouse on their profile and at the right, click on "Add to network."

   a. You'll be taken to the next stage. If you are prompted to enter an email, then enter their email if you have it.

      If you don't have their email, but you have a dialogue that gives you options such as whether you are a "colleague," "classmate," "We've done business together," "friend," "other," etc., then a good option is to select "We've done business together" and fill in the name of your current or past employer. Then click the "Send Invitation" button.

   b. Wait for them to respond to your invitation to connect. After they respond to your invitation, copy, paste and *fill in the blanks* in the script below in a message, and send to the prospect.

      Script: *"My name is_____. I've been researching the problems facing your company and your department in particular. And I have discovered a technique... that will help you [**get "emotional hot button" results or avoid "emotional hot button" problems, as found in the gold-digging research**]. Would you like me to send you the details about the technique and how I can help you implement it? If yes, kindly send me your email and postal mail box address, so that I can send both hard and electronic copies of the reports.*

      *Thanks,*

      *[Your name].*

      *P.S: Again... If you really want to [**get "emotional hot button" results or avoid "emotional hot button" problems, as found in the gold-digging research**], kindly send me your email and postal mail box address, so that I can send both hard and electronic copies of the reports.*

      *For more information about me, please click this link: [**Insert the Link to your VisualCV here**]*

8.  If you don't find "Add to network," then that person should probably be a 1ˢᵗ or 3ʳᵈ degree connection or more. (In LinkedIn, you can only add directly to your network people who are 2ⁿᵈ degree connections. 1ˢᵗ degree means they are already in your network). Simply Click on "Get Introduced."

9.  If you already have a few people in your LinkedIn network that belong to that company, you will be taken to a list of people who can get you introduced to the hiring manager.

    a.  Select the person that would do the introduction for you, and click on "Continue."

    b.  Copy, paste and *fill in the blanks* in the script above (step 7b.) in the message box for the hiring manager or hiring decision maker.

    c.  Also type in a brief message for the person doing the introduction.

    d.  Select a "Category" of subject in the drop-down box.

    e.  Type in a subject line.

    f.  Click "Send."

If after searching, you don't find them on LinkedIn, you can try contacting them on Facebook as we'll see next.

## How To Contact The Hiring Manager Or Hiring Decision Maker *Directly* On Facebook

If you don't have the phone number of the hiring manager, or you've not been able to have him/her on phone, you can contact them directly using LinkedIn as we saw previously. If you don't find them on LinkedIn, the next likely place to find them online is Facebook.

1.  Go join Facebook.com, if you've not yet done so.

2. After joining Facebook, search for the name of the person in the search box at the top of the page.

3. If you find them, click on their profile name and you'll be taken to their profile. You can send them a friend request if you wish. But it's preferable to first of all send them the script and see their response, before requesting their friendship.

4. While on their profile, click on "Message" button on the top right. You'll be taken to the message box.

5. Copy, paste and *fill in the blanks* in the script below in the message box:

Script: *"My name is_____. I've been researching the problems facing your company and your department in particular. And I have discovered a technique... that will help you [get "emotional hot button" results or avoid "emotional hot button" problems, as found in the gold-digging research]. Would you like me to send you the details about the technique and how I can help you implement it? If yes, kindly send me your email and postal mail box address, so that I can send both hard and electronic copies of the reports.*

*Thanks,*

*[Your name].*

*P.S: Again... If you really want to [get "emotional hot button" results or avoid "emotional hot button" problems, as found in the gold-digging research], kindly send me your email and postal mail box address, so that I can send both hard and electronic copies of the reports.*

*For more information about me, please click this link: [Insert the Link to your VisualCV here]*

6. Click "Send."

If after searching on Facebook, you don't find them, do everything possible to get them on phone or meet them physically in one of the places they are used to visiting and talk to them and hand them your 3MM report and interview-getting résumé.

So, let's review all what we've covered so far.

At this point, if you've been following me closely, you can see how far your passion and willingness to fit into a high-paying job, with one of the companies on your top 10 list, can bring you down your road to success.

If you've been following me and taking action, you would have done your targeting and gold-digging research and have found the real problems, frustrations, challenges and goals of the employer. Then you'd have used possibility thinking to figure out the solution to their problem.

Next, you'd have used your 3 mistakes marketing, interview-getting résumé and cover letters to influence the hiring manager, in a way that would force them to call you for an interview – once they set their eyes on your killer marketing documents (or your 3MM, interview-getting résumé and cover letters).

Now let's assume you've successfully contacted the hiring manager or hiring decision maker directly and handed them your killer 3MM and interview-getting résumé. And let's say they've finally called you for an interview. Now, the next BIG question is…

# The Job getting Formula

## STEP 5

**Can You PROVE In An Interview, That You Are Fit For The Job, Better Than Any Other Candidate? (Here Are 190 Toughest Questions And How To Answer Them)**

So, what's the interview all about? And how can one make his/her way successfully through it?

Well, this is what I can tell you:

The interview is a process where a recruiter, hiring manager or hiring decision maker tries to investigate whether you are consistent with the claims you made on paper. In other words, on paper, you look good and "attractive" as a candidate for the job. But the hiring manager, recruiter or hiring decision maker suspects it might not be so in reality. And so, they might want to interview you. And they may do this in several ways: through a phone interview, an in-person one-on-one interview or an in-person team interview.

## The Phone Interview – Why It Is Mostly A Surprise Screening Process – And How To Handle It

Although interviews are often done over the phone for one reason or another – nonetheless, phone interviews are mostly for screening purposes.

This type of screening often takes place after the hiring manager or hiring decision maker receives your marketing documents (which are your 3MM, interview-getting résumé and one or more of your interview-getting cover letters), or when the recruiter (usually from HR) receives them from the hiring manager or hiring decision maker.

The aim is to find out whether you are worth interviewing in person (or over the phone for a second time), by throwing you a few questions to quickly check your authenticity and credibility. That's why, once you hand in your marketing documents, you have to be prepared at ALL TIMES for a surprise phone interview. Once you hand in your marketing documents, the game has started. You have to be on the alert. This type of interview might even be initiated by you, on the spot, when you contact the hiring manager directly by phone to hand over your marketing documents, as we saw in Step 4.

If you sent the one-page interview-getting résumé, most of the time the phone interviewer may ask you to send an elaborate version of your one-page interview-getting résumé with details regarding your selected accomplishments, your past job responsibilities, etc. This is an opportunity to ask the interviewer which particular areas they want you to elaborate on. This is a great way to discover what their center of interest is, as regards the job.

**Warning**: DO NOT modify or provide details (both verbally or in writing) of your "fascination-style" of special skills and selected accomplishments. Those are your interview-getting weapons. If you let the cat out of the bag before it's time, you'll simply mess up all your chances of having an interview. ONLY elaborate on things like your work history and responsibilities, but make sure they are consistent with the rest of your special skills and selected accomplishments. Tell them that if they need more explanation about your skills and accomplishments, you are ready to come in for an interview to explain.

To fully prepare for a phone interview, follow the 4-step formula for predicting what will be discussed in *any* job interview, as described in the next section.

# The In-person, One-On-One Interview *Plus* The 4-Step Formula For Predicting What Will Be Discussed In ANY Interview

The next type of interview is the in-person, one-on-one interview. In this situation, the hiring manager wants to get a real world impression of who you are and what you look like – so that he/she can take time to "read" you from the way you are dressed, from the answers you provide to the questions asked, to the body language signals you show, and everything in between.

There may also be a series of one-on-one interviews in which, you are taken from one manager to the next in the company's recruitment hierarchy, e.g. from the recruiter (mostly from HR or externally) to the hiring manager and finally to the hiring decision maker or head of function/department.

Before the in-person interview, there are other impressions the interviewer will have of you, such as your declared skills and accomplishments. You have to equally manage those impressions and keep them in your favor.

Whatever the case, at the end of the process, you'll be judged from the total impressions gathered by the interviewer about you.

Did I say impressions? Yes.

Unfortunately, that's how the interview game is meant to be played – you'll be judged from impressions only, from the time the interviewer greets you to when he/she leads you back out the door.

Therefore, you'd better learn how to play this "impression game," in a way that demonstrates your personality, skills, accomplishments and experience as the best fit for solving the hiring manager's problems, with little or no objection... so that you can get the big-salary job that solves those very problems.

Now, most people INCORRECTLY think that the interview is where you come and handle the hiring manager's objections. That's why most of the time, their research starts only after they have been called for an interview. And maybe the reason they were called for interview was that… by some stroke of luck… they might have made some claims that tie in with some of the key problems of the hiring manager, but at the same time, they are usually completely ignorant of what the employer's *real* problems are.

Besides, the hiring manager might have noticed some inconsistencies in the claims on their marketing documents. But, having them as one among the few "good" candidates they could possibly find, they nonetheless call in the candidate for an interview. So, when that happens and the interview starts, the hiring manager starts "pouring" out their objections to see whether the candidate really understands the requirements of the position. This is, most often, a losing approach for the candidate – as this whole process might lead to the hiring manager discovering even more inconsistencies.

A successful interview starts long before even applying for the job, with gold-digging research that enables you to discover what the hiring manager really wants. In that way, objections can be anticipated and reduced to the greatest possible minimum.

So, successful candidates go into the interview with a deep understanding of the hiring manager's biggest fears, frustrations, challenges and goals. And it logically turns out that these are the same things that the hiring manager wants to address in the interview.

Here's the 4-step formula for predicting what will be discussed in ANY job interview.

1. Follow every step in the gold-digging and situational assessment research described in **Step 2** and find out the emotional hot buttons of the hiring manager.

2. Bring out all the pieces of information gathered about the underlying fears, frustrations, challenges and goals – in other words, the

"moving-towards" and "moving-away-from" motivators of the hiring manager.

3. Present the information gathered, in the form described in the "FearsFrustrationsGoalsChallenges-PotterExpressCo.doc" document.

   You can download the form by signing up or logging in at:

   http://jobgettingformula.com/members/signup.php. Then enter your name, email and password and click on "My Tools And Samples" tab.

4. Master how you'll describe (or articulate) all the special skills and selected accomplishments mentioned in your marketing documents to the hiring manager or interviewer. Remember, they are what made the hiring manager call you for an interview in the first place. And so, the hiring manager is expecting a detailed explanation of them.


## In-Person, Team Interview And How To Prepare

Another common type of interview is the team in-person interview. This is when you are being interviewed by a team of managers from the same department, or by a cross-functional team of managers from different departments, with each manager's opinion of you counting towards the final assessment.

The team interview can go from being a pleasant conversation to a staunch interrogation. There's usually one person, mostly from HR, chairing the questions-answers session, but in other settings, the group may agree to shoot questions at you from all angles like a group of soldiers firing heavy shots at a bunker. At the end of the interview, the interviewers, with each offering a different perspective or impression of you, would deliberate and rate your overall performance.

So, as you can see, for you to go through the interview successfully, you must know how to continue proving that you are equal or more than what is said of you in your marketing documents.

Follow the same 4-step process of preparation as in the previous section. Relax. Show confidence in your body language, and use the other techniques we'll be discussing in coming sections of this Step of the Job-getting Formula, and all will be fine.

# Four Interviewing Techniques Used By Interviewers To Assess Candidates And How To Respond To Them To Make A Powerful Positive Impression

Although most hiring managers are not formerly trained for interviewing, there are however four most common techniques used across the board, from the least experienced to the most evolved interviewer, to assess candidates. These techniques include: Behavioral Interviews, Hypothetical (or What-if) Interviews, Stress Interviews and "Let's Get It Rolling And Judging" Interviews.

## 1. Behavioral Interview Questions And The 3-Step Process For Preparing And Responding To Them

This is where the interviewer asks you questions that are solely focused on past situations, with the aim of determining how you behaved in them, such as: how you handled a particular difficult job situation that avoided or led to a negative outcome or disaster, how you reacted to a conflict with your former boss, colleague, client, member of an association, supplier, etc., or how you arrived at a particular accomplishment mentioned on your résumé. And then he/she draws facts from your conversation and makes conclusions on how you'd behave in a similar situation in the future.

Here are some examples of behavioral interview questions:

- *"Tell me about the last time you disagreed with your boss (or coworker or subordinate). What did you do, and what was the result?"*

- *"Tell me about a mistake you made."*

174

A good understanding of the hiring manager's problems (Fears, Frustrations, Challenges and Goals) will give you *most* of the clues you need to succeed with behavioral interview questions.

Here's the 3-step process to follow to successfully prepare and respond to behavioral interview questions:

1. **Go back into the past.** Walk yourself through (or recall) each of the selected accomplishments and special skills you mentioned in your marketing documents.

2. **For each accomplishment or special skill, review how you handled difficult situations**. What type of limiting work constraints did you have? What types of conflicts were involved with team members? How did you manage misunderstandings and conflicts with customers, your boss, subordinates, or colleagues? What pressing deadlines were involved and how did you manage them?

3. **Write down a story for each accomplishment and special skill you review**. Paint a picture of how and what you did, including where and when you did it, to overcome the difficulties and arrive at the accomplishment. Make sure your stories answer the questions you predicted would be discussed in the interview. The aim of writing down the story is to "wire" your brain to be prepared with the answers to possible behavioral questions linked to your accomplishments, in a very smooth and effective way.

   **Warning**: Do this 3-step review while anticipating the questions the hiring manager will be asking. I'll be sharing with you 190 of the toughest and frequently asked questions, which include some behavioral questions, in a coming section. You'll need to get the list of those questions and come back and go through this review process while, at the same time, going through the list of questions – selecting the ones you most anticipate for your interview.

2. **The Hypothetical or "What If" Interview Questions And The 3-Step Process For Preparing And Responding To Them**

In this type of questions, the interviewer imagines a particular hypothetical situation and asks you to put yourself into the picture and tell him/her how you'd react or what you'd do to get a positive outcome.

Here are some examples of hypothetical interview questions:

- *"Assuming you are responsible to put together a team for the launch of a new product we're introducing, what would you do?"*

- *"Your supervisor tells you to do something in a way you know is dead wrong. What do you do?"*

- *"Assuming you are leading a group of our salespeople who haven't met quota for the last three quarters. What would you do?"*

This hypothetical or "what-if" approach can be very dazzling to the candidate, not only because of the surprise it comes with, but also because of the requirement for you to think on your feet and formulate an accurate and satisfying answer, without counteracting the good impression the interviewer had of you from your marketing documents.

Yeah, you thought you lobbed the ball into the interviewer's court with your powerful marketing documents. Now, here's the interviewer announcing that *"the game is just starting."*

But again, a good understanding of the hiring manager's problems will give you some of the insights you need to properly anticipate and handle hypothetical interview questions.

Here's the 3-step process to follow, to successfully prepare and respond to hypothetical interview questions:

1. **Go into the future.** Imagine that you're working already for the hiring manager and putting into action each of the special skills you've listed in your marketing documents.

2. **Imagine how you'll handle difficult situations and challenges**. What types of limiting work constraints will you have? What types of conflicts will be involved with the team members? How will you manage conflicts with your new boss, colleagues or subordinates? What types of deadlines will you be dealing with, etc?

3. **Write down a story of your hypothetical imaginations.** Paint a picture of how and what you'll do, including where and when you'll do it, to overcome the possible challenges and arrive at success. Make sure your story answers the questions you predict will be discussed in the interview.

   Again, the aim of writing down the story is to "wire" your brain to be prepared with the answers to possible hypothetical questions linked to your special skills and accomplishments… in a very brilliant and confident way.

   **Warning**: Again, just as in the case of behavioral questions, you'll need to get the list of 190 questions and come back and go through this review process while, at the same time, going through the list of questions – selecting the ones you most anticipate for your interview.

**Note**: The "a-z" list of situational assessment questions we saw in Step 2 will greatly help you to understand the working environment and work constraints you'll be facing. It's advisable to interview one of your informants at length on these questions to gather vital situational or contextual information, necessary for imagining and anticipating hypothetical and behavioral questions.

### 3. The Stress Interview And Some Simple Techniques To Come Out Of It Successfully

In most jobs, the nature of the job may be very demanding or "disgusting." And also, serious clashes between people of conflicting personality types may occur in the course of doing the job. And to a great extent, this might even affect the performance of an employee who cannot cope with the stress that ensues from such a working environment.

Most employers have by now understood the reality that it is not only how qualified you are in terms of skills, knowledge and experience that's important, but also how stable, powerful and intelligent you are in managing your emotions – especially stress.

Some interviewers use stress interviews to see how an individual responds to situations of conflict. The interviewer is the one who simulates a conflict to see how the candidate would respond.

The interviewer might simply let you into the room without greeting you, look at you in a somewhat "I am disappointed in you" manner, and then ask you a question. And he/she may even ridicule your answer to the question, disagree with any further opinion of yours, stare at his watch as if you're wasting his time, and continue with a whole lot of bitter and irritating behavior.

The aim of the whole exercise is to get you off balance, emotionally. The longer you can stay calm and composed, without "breaking" into the "drama" and reacting negatively – as would be expressed in your body language – the better your chances of succeeding in the interview.

Some organizations and career experts call it your emotional energy, emotional intelligence, or intra-personal skills. Whatever the name given to it, it is simply the power to control your emotions.

Even if you're not applying to be an American Navy Seal, a military, CIA or FBI agent, you might still encounter a healthy dose of stress interview while you are involved in an ordinary job interview,

someday. This can occur, based on the conscious or unconscious
behavior of the interviewer, at some points during the interview. And the
sad fact is, he/she will use your reaction to gauge an impression of your
emotional maturity. So be prepared for it. The tricks for achieving
success in a stress interview are simple:

1.  Don't show them you're being tortured – be calm and be
    yourself.

2.  Watch the tone of your voice and your facial expression.

3.  Be mature and elevate yourself above the interviewer.

4.  Just consider it a funny game and carry some laughter about it
    inside your mind. You'll feel good and come out on the outside
    as being great.

## 4.   The "Let's Get It Rolling And Judging" Interview Approach And How To Go About It

This is the typical type of interview done by unskilled and untrained
interviewers – most hiring managers practice it unfortunately.

It typically goes like this:

The interviewer gets the ball rolling, by asking you a series of
frequently asked questions such as *"Tell me about yourself,"* then, gets
you answering them while he/she judges your responses and follows up
with other more common but often straight-forward questions like,
*"Could you take me through your entire résumé?"*

At times, the interviewer may go off on a tangent with some
boastful chatter about themselves and their accomplishments with the
company (getting you to doubt the aim of them doing so – maybe just to
satisfy their ego, or make you know how important they are, or get you
intimidated, or for some other unknown reason).

As the interview goes on, the interviewer might just be waiting to
see if you can say something about the problems they are facing and how

to solve them, in a way that makes them feel you are the right candidate for the job.

Here's the problem:

Very often, the interviewer knows what they want, but they cannot articulate it in the form of behavioral, hypothetical or other types of questions (since they have not been trained on those). So, they wait for you to take the opportunity and control the interview with what you have to say. For example, they may want to see how you'll "fit" into the team, department or organization, or how good you can collaborate with them on a personal level, in case you have to work under their supervision.

And while they are doing all that, the little they can gather from the conversation, about you, is all they have, to make a decision about whether you are competent or not. This can be often challenging and frustrating, because you won't be able to tell exactly what the interviewer wants to know.

My advice for you in such an interview is to take control of the conversational load of the interview. You'll have to do everything to explain everything, in a way that will sell your strengths despite what the interviewer does or fails to do.

## The "Interest-multiplier" Story Style For Answering Questions *Plus* 8 Reasons Why It Is More Powerful Than The "Dry" Logical Convincing Style

The Interest-multiplier story style for answering interview questions is simply a technique that is based on using short stories to showcase your strengths in multiple dimensions. It's about bundling all the different "facets" of you (selected accomplishments, special skills, qualifications, experience) into one unique story package. That is why I call it the *Interest-multiplier story style*. In other words, it multiplies your value and makes you unique in the process.

Here are 8 strong reasons why such a story is so powerful:

- **The human mind thinks in pictures.** A great story is made up of tangible, "out-there-in-the-world" pictures that one can relate to easily. Facts or information in logical form, without stories, tend to "roll off" and not stick in the mind.

- **It disarms the interviewer.** Most importantly, when you begin to tell a story, the person listening goes into "opened and relaxed" mode, their defenses come down, their "critical mind" goes to sleep and they begin picturing what you're telling them, in a receptive mode.

- **It creates great Rapport and Relevance.** When you match your story with your prospective employer's problems or challenges, it creates rapport and a deep level of connection which make them believe in you as someone who really understands and can solve their problems – just as we saw in the *Influence Weapon of "Liking"* section of the 3 Mistakes Marketing of Step 3.

- **It answers the "Who?", "What?", "When?", "Where?", "Why?" and "How?".**

When people capture facts, they tend to file them in what I refer to as the "six cabinets" of the mind. And these six filing cabinets have doors that are often labeled "Who?", "What?", "When?", "Where?", "Why?", and "How?".

When you provide information in a way that answers these six questions, such as through a carefully thought-out story, you exponentially increase your chances of being understood.

- **It gives you an EDGE of control over the rest of the interview.** As I explained previously, when you understand that people are always looking for answers to the six questions "Who?", "What?", "When?", "Where?", "Why?", and "How?", it helps you anticipate any further follow-up questions, since most of the time, more questions will be asked just to "dig deeper" and clarify one or more of these 6 questions. And in that way, studying your initial story, you can prepare other answers or stories for potential follow-up questions based on one or more of "Who?", "What?", "When?", "Where?", "Why?", or "How?" , well in advance.

- **It provides Proof.** When you tell your story with critical details, truthfulness and enthusiasm, it improves on the believability and provides proof of your competence to the interviewer.

- **It improves your communication and boosts your confidence.** When you have all your facts lined up in a story, it makes it easy to remember and helps you communicate with ease. It also increases your self-confidence and does so even more in the eyes of the interviewer.

- **It keeps a memorable picture of you in the mind of the interviewer.** After an interview, there's hardly much to be remembered by the interviewer of what a candidate said, especially if there were several candidates interviewed. A compelling and memorable story is one of the sure things that can stick in the mind of the interviewer even after you are gone.

Ok. Hope you're learning a great deal here. But I have reserved the best for last.

Now, we'll move on to learn about 190 of the TOUGHEST and frequently-asked INTERVIEW QUESTIONS, grouped in 11 categories, and the rules, techniques and formulas for answering them, starting with…

# 16 Most Common Interview Opening Questions – Why They Always Lead To *Intimidating* Follow-up Questions… And How To Prepare For Them

1.  "Tell me about yourself."

2.  "Tell me about your greatest accomplishments"

3.  "What makes you special?"

4.   "Why should I hire you?"

5.   "What are your strengths as an employee?"

6.   "How would your best friend (work colleague, boss, mother, family, etc) describe you?"

7.   "What can you do for us that someone else cannot?"

8.   "Tell me about your strongest skills."

9.   "What five adjectives best describe you?"

10.  "Tell me about your greatest personality strengths."

11.  "Why should I consider you a strong candidate for this position?"

12.  "Tell me about your greatest area of knowledge."

13.  Tell me about your last three positions. Explain what you did and how you did it, and describe the people you worked for and the people you worked with.

14.  "How would you describe your character/personality?"

15.  "What's better about you than other candidates I am interviewing?"

16.  "What were the most memorable accomplishments at your last job? (Or in your Career?)"

Yes – the preceding questions are indeed the most asked interview opening questions of all time.

But, that does not mean everybody gets over them. As a matter of fact, many people have failed their interviews just because they messed with the answers to them.

Why are interviewers fond of asking one or more of these questions at the start of the interview?

As your common sense would tell you, they want to quickly check if you're the same competent candidate that is marketed by the powerful marketing documents they received about you.

And since we are talking about competence, the interviewer is neither interested in where you were born, nor your favorite food, nor other irrelevant information. So, don't tell them about that.

The easiest way to shorten an interview, and save the interviewer time, is to mess up the answers to these common opening questions.

If you say that's not what you want, then here's how to make the interviewer stay with you longer.

You have to say something in the light of "Here's what I have achieved and what I can do for you if you offer me the job."

For example: *"In 2010, while I was working as Sales Director at Best-Selling-Shop, I discovered how to make people spend money in one single store more than they do in five, and I thought I could share the same formula with you if you offer me the job. What do you think about that?"*

Then the interviewer might say *"Hmmm that's interesting... can you explain..."*

I guess you see where that's leading to? Obviously, it opens the door to the next question.

Note: It's so important to end your answers with an engaging question to the interviewer, especially at the start of the interview.

Why?

Well, it's simple. You want to help warm up the interviewer. You don't have any clue, at this point, about the interviewing skills of the interviewer. And so, you don't want to lend your fate to an inexperienced interviewer, hoping that they'll be engaged throughout the rest of the interview... and only to find out at the end that, you didn't have the right questions to sell yourself well.

Remember, you've worked very hard to get to this point of getting the high-paying job you want, and you don't want to let the most expected type of questions stop you from moving ahead to an eventual job offer.

## How To Prepare For Interview-Opening Questions

As an example of someone who has made their way up to the interview, let's assume you're the owner of the interview-getting résumé named "Interview-gettingRésuméExample1.pdf", which you can download (by entering your name, email address and password) at:

http://jobgettingformula.com/members/signup.php, and clicking on "My Tools And Samples" tab.

Also download the file named **"Converting Tasks And Projects To Accomplishments Examples.pdf"** – this is the worksheet that was used to create that powerful, interview-getting résumé, which we'll assume for illustrative purposes got you the interview.

Like I recommend you do for all other types of interview questions, you have to prepare for the opening questions before the interview.

Here are the 5 steps to prepare for interview opening questions:

a.  Revisit the details on your résumé.

b.  Focus on your "Work History," "Selected Accomplishments," "Special Skills," "Professional Trainings," and other sections of your résumé that you think are relevant to the job and which you suspect have caused the employer to call you for an interview. Create a short interest-multiplier story outline that touches on all sections of your résumé that are relevant to the job.

c.  Take this list of interview-opening questions through the 3-step review process for behavioral and hypothetical questions, respectively.

d.  Articulate your skills, accomplishments, professional training, and work history around the hiring manager's "moving-towards" and "moving-away-from" motivators.

e.  Here's an example, using the résumé you downloaded. (I have highlighted in **bold** the hiring manager's "moving-towards" and "moving-away-from" motivators, so you can see how they have been properly articulated):

*"In 2001, after completing my MBA in Banking and Finance, I started my career with US Bank where I worked as Senior Accounts Executive for 7 years. In my first 3 years of office, **I led a major project that boosted the bank's sales by an average of 28% and brought an extra 2 million dollars in revenue. This was achieved through identifying, testing and introducing special new products to meet customers' needs.***

*Then later on, in my last four years with the same bank, **I initiated and managed the use of special ATMs, as marketing and advertising platforms, to deliver carefully coordinated, high-impact loan product campaigns that increased sales by 6 million dollars and reduced marketing spending by an average of 17%.***

*In late 2007, I joined Wells Fargo Bank, where I have been working for the past 3 years as National Accounts manager. **One of the key projects that I am really proud of is that of acquiring Wal-Mart's account from one of our major competitors (Bank of America), by beating them in a Request for Proposal (RFP). I led and guided the team on the drafting and compiling of the RFP response documents, and used my relationship-building skills to close a deal that grew the bank's sales by 26%.***

***In my 10 years of continuously helping to grow sales** for my present and past employers, I have developed some **unique skills that would give me an edge in delivering the same type of growth to ABC Bank**. They include:*

- *How to use **little-known "Inspirational Leadership" techniques to motivate and encourage team members** to take on **higher levels of responsibility, exceed goals** and **beat deadlines.***

- *A 7-step Strategy for carrying out good market research, analysis and competitive intelligence... and how to deploy new product development accordingly.*

- *How to use influential and persuasive communication to develop strong business relationships with clients and how to write and compile RFP Submissions that win BIG contracts.*

*I am excited to have this interview opportunity to discuss how this job will enable me to learn new skills as well as develop my strengths further, while delivering growth to the business.*

*I learned that ABC is losing market share. Are there any other challenges with growing ABC Bank's sales you'd like me to know?*

**Some key points to note that would guide you:**

- If you do a proper rehearsal, this whole opening story of yours can take a maximum of 2 minutes. Anything above 2 minutes is considered long and boring. The key point anyway is to make sure it's articulated about the hiring manager's moving-towards and moving-away-from motivators.

- You don't have to recite your résumé word-for-word. Look at how *cleverly* the selected accomplishments, special skills, work history and education are articulated in this example opening interest-multiplier story.

- Notice the use of 100-dollar words to describe accomplishments such as "initiated," "managed," "led," "boosted," etc. Take time to choose your words.

- You have to recite your story to the point where you can comfortably keep eye contact with the interviewer and speak in a conversational manner, so that it won't seem like you're reciting your résumé.

- Have proofs such as printed recommendations, testimonials, recognitions, awards, certificates, work samples, etc., handy and ready to show, to back up your accomplishments.

- By ending your story with a question about the key issues the employer is facing, it shows you know the employer's problems, and that goes to answer **Big Question #2** of the Job-getting Formula (which basically asks, *"Do you know the prospective employer's PROBLEMS and ASPIRATIONS better than any other candidate?"*). This would increase your score dramatically. It also helps you keep track of the interview by finding out, confirming, and gaining agreement with the interviewer on the big problems of the employer.

- By enthusiastically saying that you're excited about having the job as an opportunity to learn new skills as well as develop your strengths further, while delivering growth to the business, it shows the interviewer your passion and willingness to do the job, thereby validating **Big Question #1** of the Job-getting Formula (which asks, *"Are you PASSIONATE and WILLING to fit into the high-paying job more than any other candidate?"*)

- Preparing your opening interest-multiplier story, by writing it down like this in advance, gets you ready for the other variations of opening questions such as, *"Tell me about your greatest accomplishments," "Tell me about your strongest skills," "Tell me about your greatest area of knowledge," "Why should I hire you?"* etc. All you have to do is to adjust your response accordingly.

As examples:

- If you are asked *"What makes you special?"* or *"Why should I hire you?"*, you can simply start by saying *"I bring along some unique strengths to this position, based on the combination of my accomplishments, qualification, experience and special skills..."* and then continue with the same type of phrasing and articulations, as in the example story.

- If you are asked *"What five adjectives best describe you?"* you can simply respond by saying *"Well, in order for you to understand what 5 adjectives best describes me, I would like to give you a rundown of the special skills I have developed that best describe me..."* and continue with the same type of articulations as in the example story.

  **Note**: The general rule for answering the different opening questions is always: Be creative in phrasing and articulating your story and talk about yourself in the light of the employer's "what's in it for me." Don't get distracted into talking about irrelevant details about you. That would only offer the interview more opportunities to drag you into the mud. As a matter of fact, your answers would always determine the direction of the interview.

- Giving a high-level rundown of your selected accomplishments, special skills, employment history, education, and other relevant details would score you many points, but the game is just starting, so you have to keep focused on follow-up questions that are aimed at checking whether you can really deliver results, as you claim. The interviewer is ready to go the extra mile to find out if you can successfully pass **Big Question #3** of the Job-getting Formula, which is: *"Can you DELIVER RESULTS, despite on-the-job challenges, better than any other candidate?"*

- Presenting a high-level description of your special skills and accomplishments is also a powerful way to control the interview – this enables you to anticipate possible follow up questions that the interviewer may ask, such as:

  o *"Can you explain to me, step-by-step, how you boosted sales by 28%?"*

  o *"Can you tell us a bit about your 7-step Strategy for carrying out good market research, analysis and competitive intelligence...?"*

o *"What makes you think that you can deliver the same results to us?"*

o *"Tell me how you used influential and persuasive communication to create relationships that 'moved' clients to sign BIG contracts..."*

o *"Explain how you led the team to deliver the results you just mentioned..."*

o *"Explain how you closed the deal..."*

o *"Can you tell us a bit about your 'little known' inspirational leadership techniques to motivate your team members?"*

o *Etc.*

## How To Anticipate And Prepare For Follow-up Questions

a. Revisit the details in the **<u>"Converting Tasks And Projects To Accomplishments Examples.pdf"</u>** worksheet.

b. Focus on the 'How' and 'Accomplishment' columns. (You'll realize that it's on the 'How' column of this worksheet that we recorded the details of the projects or tasks we used to develop the résumé.)

c. Anticipate and create short stories for possible follow up questions.

d. Example:

Let's look in the 'Accomplishment' column of the worksheet for the accomplishment that says: *"Boosted sales of major bank by 28% and brought in extra $2 million in revenues by identifying, testing and introducing special new products to meet customers' needs (June 2001 – July 2003, US Bank)."*

Let's assume you anticipate that the interviewer may ask, *"Can
you explain to me, step-by-step, how you boosted sales by
28%?"*

How would you prepare?

It's simple. You prepare a short story by looking at the details
you wrote in the 'How' column (still assuming you are the
owner of this résumé and the notes on the worksheet – I'd advise
that you follow the same approach and do the same). Here are
the details:

---

- Was project leader for project BOOST.

- Introduced the idea of the 'Special Loans
  Package'

- I presented details of project idea to Exec
  members, and they ordered a pilot phase to test
  initiative.

- Did test and results were good and promising,
  and that led to Exec members validating
  project roll out.

- This special loans offer was made to all
  existing clients and a great majority subscribed
  to it.

- $2 million was reported to have been brought
  in by this special loan product initiative and
  this corresponded to a 28% increase in sales.

---

Use these details (obviously not those of this case study – but as jotted
down for your own case), and carefully write out your stories.

# How Can Some Of Your Weaknesses Affect The Job? (<u>Warning</u>: What NEVER To Say When You Are Asked About Your Weaknesses And How To Turn Your Weaknesses Into Strengths)

17. "What's your greatest weakness?"

18. "What's the biggest failure you've had in your career? What steps have you taken to make sure something like that doesn't happen again?"

19. "If you could change one thing about your personality just by snapping your fingers, what would it be and why?"

20. "Tell me about the one thing in your life you're most ashamed of?"

21. "What skills do you most need to develop or acquire in order to advance your career?"

22. "What does your supervisor tend to criticize about your performance (or attitude)?"

23. "What aspect of your personality/attitude do you consider a weakness?"

24. "What's your biggest disadvantage?"

I don't know how it feels like for you, but from my personal experience, I have noticed that it is usually very difficult to notice and accept our weaknesses. That's why going into an interview without a clue about how to answer this type of weakness-focused questions can be a losing bargain for any candidate.

Here's what NEVER to say:

NEVER declare in an interview that you have no weaknesses. This might just put an end to the interview.

I remember one time when I was in the middle of an interview, I was asked to say what my weaknesses were. I got tongue-tied, hemming and hawing. In short, it was awful and embarrassing. And worst of all, I said something similar to "I don't have any weakness" - and that, I am sure, was one of the causes, if not the major cause, of me not getting the job.

But for you, there is good news. There's a way I have found that you can talk about your weaknesses that would give them 2 dimensions – a weakness that if "flipped" around may be perceived as a strength.

I call this technique the "**double-edged sword**" technique, because when the interviewer asks you a weakness-focused question, they are relying only on the one edge of the "sword" that's pointing towards your weaknesses. But this technique helps you find the other edge of the sword pointing "towards" the positive side of the weakness.

This technique is based on the premise that failure in any action that was intended for "good" always carries a learning opportunity. And a learning point means an experience that can be packaged in a well-worded story and sold to an interviewer.

Here are some examples:

- Let's say your weakness is that you focus too much on details. Then you can say: *"In most of my meetings a couple of years ago, when presenting a suggestion, I used to focus on the details, and this made most of my suggestions boring and less attractive to my team members. Since realizing this, I have discovered a presentation technique on how to introduce suggestions in a way that incites the listener to ask for the details. In that way I can only talk about the details if they ask for them."*

- Let's assume another weakness of yours is inflexibility with plans. You can say: *"Early on in my career, I used to be inflexible with plans and schedules of projects, thinking that changes in plans may cause delays. And though this has helped me keep to some tight deadlines, it has equally made me miss solving some problems that required a few tweaks on the initial plan. Since that time, I've vowed to stop being inflexible with plans while making sure I do everything to meet deadlines."*

**Warning**: Prepare for this type of questions in advance and use them as an opportunity to demonstrate strengths or experiences acquired through temporary failures or weaknesses.

The formula for phrasing your stories when using the "double-edged sword" technique should simply be:

[Failure caused by my weakness while aiming at a worthy goal] + [Lessons learned] + [How I became stronger as a result]

Try to place the failure far back in your career history. And also try to avoid discussing failures that are related to key aspects of the job. This is so that, if by accident, you give a less convincing answer, the doubts in the interviewer's mind would not put to question your ability to tackle the major aspects of the job.

Ok. Great! So far, we've covered some powerful interview secrets that might take you very far towards creating a successful interview.

But, if the interviewer is still not fully convinced about your capabilities or is simply not done with investigating your strong and weak points, then… they may introduce any of the next set of questions that "probe" into *behavioral specifics* (or behavioral questions) relating to particular past failures or negative situations in your career.

## What Did You Learn (*or Failed To Learn*) From Past Failures? How Can That Affect The Job?

25. "Tell me about a mistake you made."

26. "Tell me about the worst decision you ever made."

27. "Tell me about the last time you were frustrated at work."

28. "Tell me about the last time you failed to meet your boss's expectation"

29. "Tell me about the last time you made a lost sale."

30. "Tell me about the last time you dealt with a difficult colleague."

31. "Tell me about the last time you were denied a promotion."

32. "Tell me about the last time you failed to complete a project on time."

33. "Tell me about the last time you had to make an unpopular decision."

34. "Tell me about the last time you dealt with a difficult customer."

35. "Tell me about the last time you dealt with a difficult boss."

36. "Tell me about the last time you dealt with a difficult subordinate."

37. "What's the most difficult part of being a manager (or an executive)?"

38. "What kinds of decisions are difficult for you to make?"

39. "Tell me about the last time you lost your temper."

40. "You've had little experience with budgeting (or sales or whatever). How do you intend to learn what you need to know to perform in this job?"

41. "Tell me about the last time you disagreed with your boss/coworker/subordinate. What did you do, and what was the result?"

42. "Tell me about the last time you were fired or laid off."

43. "Tell me about the last time you went over budget."

44. "Tell me about the last time you took a risk. Was it the right decision? What would you have done differently?"


So, how do you prepare for such questions and how do you answer them?

The first thing to note is that these are all behavioral questions and most of them are subjecting you to a specific negative past situation, to find out what you learned from it. They are focused on the specifics about lessons learned.

The general rule for these types of questions is to answer them in the same way you'd answer a "What's your greatest weakness?" question, which is, using the double-edged sword technique, but with more specifics.

So, use the double-edged sword technique:

[Failure caused by my weakness while aiming at a worthy goal] + [Lessons learned] + [How I became stronger as a result],

Follow the guidelines in the 3-step process for preparing behavioral questions, as we saw in a previous section. But put your answer in a story that shows, specifically:

1. The context or the situation and considerations.

2. What you did wrong.

3. Where you did it.

4. When you did it.

5. Why or what pushed you to do it.

6. What lessons did you learn?

7. How do you want to use that valuable experience going forward?

With almost all these questions, the interviewer assumes that the situations referred to are those you must have experienced, and very often they are right.

If however, you are asked about something you've never done, simply say you haven't experienced such a thing before. But be careful, it may just be the most important experiential requirement for the job. That's why I always advise you to do proper gold-digging research about the company, as a prime prerequisite for success with the interview and getting the job.

Another point to note is that these types of questions can help the interviewer to discover inconsistencies with what you've previously said in the interview. Therefore, be careful how you lay out your specifics. The best way to handle this is to anticipate questions like these in relation to specific requirements of the job and prepare consistent answers to them before the interview.

But all this may not be sufficient.

The interviewer may not be entirely satisfied with your performance yet, and so they may continue with other questions relating to the BIG question of *"Can you DELIVER RESULTS, despite on-the-job challenges, better than any other candidate?"* – remember the famous Question #3 of the Job-getting Formula.

That may lead us to the next set of questions.

## Can You Really Show Me That You Have The Required Skills, Attitude And Experience To Deliver Results?

45. "What do you do when you're having trouble solving a problem?"

46. "What do you do when you're having trouble with a colleague/boss/subordinate?"

47. "Tell me about the last time you saved your company money."

48. "Tell me about the last time you helped grow sales."

49. "Tell me about the last time you found a unique solution to a problem."

50. "Tell me about the last time you found a cost-effective solution to a problem."

51. "Tell me about the last time you fired someone. Why?"

52. "Tell me about the last time you learned a new skill."

53. "Do you anticipate problems well or merely react to them?"

54. "Tell me about the last time you hired someone."

55. "Have you ever hired anyone? Why did you choose them?"

56. "Are you a risk-taker or do you prefer to play it safe?"

57. "How do you generally handle conflict?"

58. "How do you motivate people?"

59. "What do you do when you're having trouble with your job?"

60. "What do you do when things are slow?"

61. "Are you bilingual?"

62. "What other languages do you speak apart from English (or French or Spanish)?"

63. "Have you managed people in any of the positions you've held?"

64. "Have you been in charge of budgeting (or approving expenses, monitoring departmental progress against goals, etc)? How qualified and experienced are you in this area?"

65. "Did you inaugurate new procedures/systems/policies/etc in your previous position? Tell me about them."

66. "What do you do when things are hectic?"

67. "What do you do when you have multiple priorities (family work/school/etc.)?"

68. "How do you deal with subordinates who are part of the problem rather than part of the solution?"

69. "See that picture frame on the wall? Sell it to me."

70. "Have you ever organized a marketing campaign?"

71. "Tell me about the last time you solved/repaired a machine breakdown or problem."

72. "Describe the way your department is organized. Also, what is the title of the person to whom you report? What are his or her exact responsibilities?"

73. "How do you handle change?"

74. "How do you go about making important decisions?"

75. "Are you an organized person? (Or how organized are you?)"

76. "Do you work well under pressure?"

77. "Tell me about the first two hours of your typical day."

78. "Do you manage your time well? (Or how do you manage your time?)"

79. "Your supervisor tells you to do something in a way you know is dead wrong. What do you do?"

80. "If you were unfairly criticized by your supervisor, what would you do?"

81. "Your supervisor left an assignment in your in-box, and then went on vacation for three weeks. You can't reach him/her, and you don't fully understand the assignment. What do you do?"

82. "Your best friend constantly borrows money from petty cash and fails to return it. You've spoken to her, and she just laughs at you. What do you do?"

83. "Assuming you are responsible to put together a team for the launch of a new product we're introducing, what would you do?"

84. "Assuming you are leading a group of our salespeople who haven't met quota for the last three quarters, what would you do?"

Most of these questions are obviously questions aimed at testing your problem-solving skills like attitude, leadership, ability to learn from situations and from others, humility to ask for help, personal initiative, creativity, organizational skills, how you manage conflict, respect for hierarchy, ability to adapt to change, how you consider company vs. personal interests, expertise and technical know-how, teamwork and collaboration, how logically or emotionally you make decisions, knowledge about the challenges of the job, etc.

At this point in the interview, the interviewer would be trying to test your job-related and problem-solving skills, by placing you in the face of a problem, adversity or real-life job situation and observe how you'd respond.

The interviewer may also want to rephrase some of the previously asked questions to catch possible inconsistencies in your declarations.

Always remember that skills are developed and used to solve problems. The best way an interviewer can test your skills is to get you face-to-face with a specific type of problem. Some of the questions may be behavioral or hypothetical in nature.

If you have some proof of competence in the form of work samples, testimonials, recommendations, presentations, awards, trophies, etc., then this is one of the best moments to show them as you speak, in order to remove some doubts and boost your credibility.

Focus on the skills and accomplishment sections of your résumé. These are mostly the sections that are being tested here.

For example, let's say you are asked *"What do you do when you're having trouble with a subordinate?"* You may be asked this because you either said somewhere in your résumé that you are great at interacting with people (or that you're a great team player). Even if you didn't mention it in your résumé, the interviewer may still ask you this question, if "getting along with people" is a key skill for the job. You see what I mean?

Here's my recommended course of action for you:

- Do in-depth research about the functional and leadership
requirements of the job – by using the gold-digging and situational
assessment questions discussed in Step 2, to capture relevant
information about the job, the department, the company, their
customers, suppliers, competitors, etc.

- Visualize or imagine the interviewer drilling you to investigate all
the skills and accomplishment claims you've made in your résumé as
well as those related to the job. You can do this by simply following
the 3-step process for preparing behavioral and hypothetical
questions, as we saw earlier.

- Use this list of 40 questions (from question 45 to 84) to kick-start
your visualization and anticipation; and see yourself providing the
right answers. Write down the answers that come to mind.

- Prepare short interest multiplier stories for them with specifics before
the interview. Even one or two-sentence stories may still work. So
don't consider this a huge task – do it! You'll be very glad you did.

If you do this visualization and anticipation exercise, and if you've
been through a forgotten experience in the past, where you've
consciously or unconsciously developed a skill related to any question,
then as if by "magic," you'll get a great answer for that question before
the interview. You might also get answers to *unexpected* questions about
your skills, even in the middle of the interview.

So, you don't have to worry too much if you don't get all the
answers, or if you don't answer all the questions before going into the
interview. Be confident and go through all the questions several times
and brainstorm answers to them. Just by *repeatedly* going through the
questions, you will *subconsciously* program your mind to be ready with
answers.

The reason for this is that, your reticular activating system (the
RAS) of your brain (that I won't touch on in detail here), will be
programmed to filter all information coming into your conscious mind
and will search only for information related to the questions you were

visualizing before the interview. All you need to do is to trust your RAS, which can be activated through focused concentration and frequent contemplation over this list of questions. This is very powerful. Trust me.

Ok. Now to the next set of questions.

The interviewer may also be interested in finding out how well you know about their company and the problems and challenges they are facing.

They may then ask you the next set of questions, in line with Big Question #2 of the Job-getting Formula – *"Do you know the prospective employer's PROBLEMS and ASPIRATIONS better than any other candidate?"*

## How Much Do You Know About Our Company's Problems In Relation To The Job?

85. "How much do you know about our company?"

86. "Do you have any questions?"

87. "What have you heard about our company that you don't like?"

88. "This is a much smaller company than you've worked for. How do you feel about that?"

89. "Who do you think are our two (or three or five) major competitors?"

90. "Which of our new products do you think has the greatest potential for growth?"

91. "What do you think is the greatest challenge facing our company/industry?"

92. "This is a much larger company than you've worked for. How do you feel about that?"

This is where your gold-digging and situational assessment research will save you.

If you are asked whether you have any questions, NEVER say you have no questions. That would immediately tell the interviewer that you didn't do any in-depth research about their company and its problems in relation to the job – and hence you're neither very much interested in, nor fit for the position.

If you had mastered the problem of the employer, then you'd be asking very pertinent and engaging questions at this point... in a way that would boost your chances of being hired.

As an example, consider 3 candidates competing for a position of Chief Accountant.

The first asks no question.

The second asks, *"How many candidates are competing for this position?"*

The third asks *"From my research I heard that your company is about to install a new companywide data management software that would dramatically change the way you do business in the company. Are there any challenges you're anticipating that would be faced by the selected candidate? Are there measures being taken, such as adequate training of staff, to enable a smooth transition?"*

All other things being equal, which of the 3 candidates would you select, if you are the Finance Director of the company?

No doubt about it. I'd select the third candidate. Their interest and knowledge about the employer's challenges are very obvious.

Again, the rule is: NEVER say you don't have questions or you don't know anything about the employer's company.

Here's another tricky question: *"What have you heard about our company that you don't like?"*

You might be tempted to say I don't know anything negative or I haven't heard anything I don't like about your company. Guess what? That's a loser.

Again if you've done your research well, this is another golden opportunity to break out from the crowd, by saying something like, *"I learned that you guys are losing market share to your major competitor. That really bothers me because I've recently discovered some great market share recovery strategies that can help."* You get the idea?

After discovering that there's a high likelihood of you being capable of delivering results, the interviewer may want to find out more about your personality by asking you one or more questions in the next category.

## Let's See The Things You're Interested In, To Further Discover Your Passion And True Personality

93. "What's the last book you read?"

94. "What's the last movie you watched?"

95. "What three people would you most like to have dinner with?"

96. "Which other person would you invite to a desert island?"

97. "What's your favorite book?"

98. "Who's your favorite actor?"

99. "What's your favorite TV show?"

100. "What magazines do you read regularly?"

101. "Where do you get your news?"

102. "Why did you choose to work for your present employer?"

Often, experienced interviewers would use your interests to deduce where your *natural* focus and passion lies. They do this by asking you a series of *"Why are you interested in X?"* questions. Then, they'll gather some of your areas of interest to gauge an impression of what might be your personality type and natural preferences.

The general rule that works for answering these types of questions is to use **"My Interests Match the Job"** technique as follows:

[I made "X choice" because of "Y reason"] + [This is what I discovered in the process] + [This is how the "Y reason" matches the job I am now interviewing for]

Example: Let's assume you're interviewing for a marketing position and your favorite show is the weight loss TV show entitled – "The Best Loser." And you're asked *"What's your favorite TV show?"*

You can say: *"My favorite show is The Best Loser, not just because I like to gain knowledge and inspiration about keeping good health, but also because of the great advertising that's being aired during the show. I learn a lot about marketing communication in those advertisements, and some of what I have learned would be very critical to this new job."*

If you happen to reach this stage of the interview, be grateful and be proud of yourself and your great pre-interview preparation. As you'll notice, pre-interview preparation pays big dividends, by moving you closer and closer to a possible high-paying job offer.

But since you're not there yet, don't let the excitement take you off course. Stay relaxed and study this next set of questions, which is geared towards your personal compatibility with the job and the people you'll be working with.

Next...

# Are Your Personal Style, Attitude And Goals Compatible With Those Of Our Team (or The Organization You'll Be Working For)?

103. "What do you want to be doing three years from now?"

104. "Based on what you know about our industry, how is your "ideal job" related to the description of the job for which you're interviewing?"

105. "Where do you see yourself five years from now?"

106. "Would you like to have your boss' job? Why or why not?"

107. "Tell me the types of people you have trouble getting along with"

108. "What aspects of the job I have described appeal to you?"

109. "If you could go as far as your abilities would take you in a fast growing company, where would that be, and how quickly?"

110. "What was the most satisfying position you held and why?"

111. "If you could start your career over again, what would you do differently?"

112. "What was your favorite job? Why?"

113. "Tell me about the best/worst boss you ever had."

114. "What are your most important long term goals?"

115. "Have you recently established any personal objectives or goals?

116. "What does growth mean to you?"

117. "Do you prefer to work by yourself or with others?"

118. "What do you want to do with your life?"

119. "Describe your management philosophy."

120. "What does success mean to you?"

121. "What does failure mean to you?"

122. "What does challenge mean to you?"

123. "What does problem mean to you?"

124. "What are you looking for in your next job?"

125. "If you could have any job in the world, what would it be?"

126. "If you could work for any company in the world, which would it be?"

127. "What do you feel an employer owes an employee?"

128. "The successful candidate for this position will be working with some highly trained individuals who have been with the company for a long time. How will you mesh with them?

129. "Are you willing to travel?"

130. "Are you willing to relocate?"

131. "Will travel be a burden on your family?"

132. "How will you handle the least interesting or most unpleasant parts of this job?"

133. "How long do you plan to stay with us?

The reason for these types of questions is to check whether you are compatible with the team and the work culture - whether your vision and goals are compatible with that of the company and if your personal and management style fits in.

If the interviewer is the hiring manager, he/she may want to check if you'll be a good personality match.

The following are guidelines and examples for answering these questions:

- Do proper research about the personality type of the manager and the culture of the department and company before the interview. Use the situational assessment questions discussed in Step 2 to capture key information, which will help you shape your answers.

- Make sure your goals and vision are compatible with that of the employer or hiring manager. For example, let's say you are asked: *"Where do you see yourself five years from now?"* You might say: *"I am really interested in contributing to the company's growth or solving the company's problem."* (But be specific by talking in terms of the job in question). And continue by saying: *"I know that if I achieve that goal, then for a company that is growing, I'll find personal growth opportunities along similar or related career paths within the company, in the near future."*

  **Warning**: DO NOT say you want to take the position of the hiring manager in the next five years. Though you'd sound ambitious, that might not be to the taste of the hiring manager – allow the hiring manager to tell you if they eventually want you to take their position.

- If you were asked a tricky question like, *"If you could start your career over again, what would you do differently?"*

  Be careful what you say. Do not say I would have taken a course in film-making when the job you are interviewing for is in accounting. If you do, the interviewer will immediately deduce that though you may be good for the job, you are certainly not passionate about it and so you won't be ready to go the extra mile to get results. In this case, you'd be in direct violation of Big Question #1 of the Job-getting Formula, which says *"Are you PASSIONATE and WILLING to fit into the high-paying job more than any other candidate?"*

  In this case, you can say, if you had such an opportunity, you'd take a course that would help you achieve the goals that are related to the job you're interviewing for.

- If you are asked, *"Tell me about the best/worst boss you ever had"* and you are being interviewed by the hiring manger, then make sure your description of your *best* boss matches that of the boss that was described to you in your research – that of the future boss who is sitting across the desk from you and interviewing you.

So, what would you say about your *worst* boss?

Talk about your worst boss using the double-edged sword technique. Say how their somewhat "negative" character made you grow stronger.

**Warning**: As a general rule, never blame a former boss or colleague in an interview. That would only spill out bad vibes that may make the interviewer think that your own negativity might be part of the problem.

● Use "My Interests Match the Job" technique for questions that have to do with your *personal choice* or *preference* such as:

*"If you could work for any company in the world, which would it be?"*, *"What are your most important long term goals?"*, *"What does challenge mean to you?"*, etc.

Here are some examples:

If you're asked what challenge means to you, you can say:

*"For me, challenge means an opportunity to take all that I have learned, including my leadership, teamwork, collaboration, creativity and personal initiative, to find solutions to problems."*

Or, if you're interviewing for a position that has much to do with 'Consultative Selling', and you're asked: *"If you could work for any company in the world, which would it be?"*, you can say:

*"If I could work for any company in the world, I would look for one that offers opportunities for growth, especially in 'consultative selling,' because that has been my passion for quite some time now."*

Now, let's move to the next set of possible questions.

Every employer knows that job seekers always have their 'personal agenda" with regards to the job they're applying for. So, an experienced or well-trained interviewer would want to find out yours with the next set of questions.

# What Other "Hidden" Motives/Intentions Are Attracting You To This Job?

134. "You've changed jobs quite frequently. How do we know you'll stick around?"

135. "You've been with your current employer for only a short amount of time. Is that an indication that you'll be moving around a lot throughout your career?"

136. "You've been with the same organization for 15 years. Won't you have a tough time getting used to a new culture, company, atmosphere, team, organization?"

137. "Why are you thinking of leaving your current job?"

138. "Where does your boss think you are right now?"

139. "If you have complaints about your current job/boss/company, why haven't you brought your concerns to their attention?"

140. "If you don't leave your current job, what will happen there? How far do you expect to advance?"

141. "If you're so happy at your current job, why are you leaving? Will they be surprised?"

142. "What would have to change at your current job to make it tenable?"

As you may notice, all of these questions are somehow checking your "hidden" motives or intentions – in other words, your hidden "selfish" interests.

The best technique to use to answer them is the "My Interests Match the Job" technique.

Here are some examples using "My Interests Match the Job" technique:

- If you're asked, *"Why are you thinking of leaving your current job?"*

  You can say: *"I know it's a difficult decision to leave my current job, and one which would not be liked by my present boss. But for the time being, the opportunities for growth in my current job are not as interesting as the one offered by your company. While my present role is limited strictly to brand marketing, the role you are offering provides an additional cross-functional role with the manufacturing department, for new product development projects."*

  **Warning:** DO NOT say you're moving because the job for which you're interviewing promises to pay higher.

- If you're asked, *"You've changed jobs quite frequently. How do we know you'll stick around?"*

  You can say: *"Initially in my career, my main interest in changing jobs was to find something I was really passionate about. Since I got my last job as Supply Analyst for my present employer, I have found that working as Supply Analyst is really what I was meant to do, as I really enjoy it. This new position of Senior Supply Analyst will give me more responsibilities and stability to grow in this field."*

Notice how My Interests Match the Job technique applies:

[I made "X choice" because of "Y reason"] + [This is what I discovered in the process] + [This is how "Y reason" matches the job I am now interviewing for]

Rather than giving you an answer for each question, I prefer to give you the formulas and rules for answering them. Remember the saying: *"Give someone a fish and feed him for a day, but teach him how to fish and feed him for a lifetime."*

When you practice and master these rules and formulas, you'll be able to ace every job interview in your field of knowledge and experience.

And now, let's move to the next set of questions that usually come towards the end of an interview, which is already going successfully…

## Yes, You Are Great! But Are You Fit For The Job In A Cost-effective Way?

143. "Are you in good health? What do you do to stay in shape?"

144. "Are you pregnant?"

145. "Do you intend to have children in the near future?"

146. "Do you have any physical problems that may limit your ability to perform this job? If so, what accommodations would be necessary?"

147. "When were you last in the hospital?"

148. "Do you have any health problems?"

149. "How's your back?"

150. "Were you ever denied health/life insurance?"

151. "Do you spend a lot on prescriptions?"

152. "How do you manage to balance career and family?"

153. "What do you like to do when you're not at work?"

154. "What are your hobbies?"

155. "What do you like to do during your off-hours?"

Why on earth would an interviewer ask you such questions?

Well, if your interviewer is someone from HR whose goal is to fulfill company policy of cost-effective hiring or is a hiring manager who is conscious of this policy, then you may be asked one or more of these questions.

The general rule is to focus on the concerns of the interviewer and explain to them why and how you think their concerns are no "big deal," and can be easily taken care of by you. Avoid giving the interviewer any information that can be used against you.

For example, let's assume you're asked *"Do you have back pain? And do you spend a lot on prescriptions?"*

And you know that although you might have back pain, that does not affect your ability to do the job, then simply say, *"If your concern is whether I am able to do the job, my answer is simple. Yes, I can do the job."*

Note that no mention is made about whether or not you have back pain in your answer to the question. This would make it *difficult* for the interviewer to simply record that "you said you had back pain" as a reason to "disqualify" you. If they do, they might be doing that at their own legal risk.

But let's say you're asked *"What's your hobby?"* and you say you always attend night parties every Sunday. The interviewer may doubt your being physically fit to work on Mondays.

As I said before, the rule for these questions is always to give out information about you that would not raise question marks or would not be used against you.

As a general rule, if you do your research well, you'd be able to easily anticipate and find good answers for any of such questions, in a way that would be relevant to the job.

However, if the interviewer clearly notices a personal condition, such as a pregnancy, which might impact negatively on the job in terms of maternity leave, and which is obviously unavoidable, then they may use that to disqualify the candidate without necessarily letting him/her know. And there's nothing to do about it.

Next...

# Let's See How Much Further You Can Fit Into The Real Culture. (Who Cares If You Think Of It As Being Discriminatory Or Illegal?)

156. "How old are you?"

157. "When were you born?"

158. "When did you graduate from high school?"

159. "Are you near retirement age?"

160. "Aren't you a little young to be seeking a job with this much responsibility?"

161. "Aren't you a little too old for a fast-paced company such as ours?"

162. "Are you single (married, separated, divorced)?"

163. "Do you live alone?"

164. "Do you have any children?"

165. "Are you a single parent?"

166. "How do I address you? Mrs./Miss/Ms?"

167. "How much time do you spend with your family?"

168. "Tell me about your children."

169. "Do you live with your parents?"

170. "What childcare arrangements have you made for your children?"

171. "My wife hates me working on weekends. What about yours?"

172. "Are you a family man (woman)?"

173. "What's your nationality?"

174. "Where your parents born in this country?"

175. "Were you born in this country?"

176. "What kind of accent is that?"

177. "Where were you born?"

178. "What's your sexual orientation?"

179. "Are you straight? (Are you gay? or do you date other men? or do you date other women?)"

180. "Are you Jewish/Christian/Buddhist/etc?"

181. "We're a Christian/Jewish/Muslim firm. Will that be a problem for you?"

182. "Do you have any other source of income?"

183. "Do you earn money from hobbies or investments?"

184. "Have you ever been arrested?"

In some countries (or states), some of these questions are legally correct to ask in an interview, while in others, they are not. It's always good to know what the laws of your country or state provide for such questions.

If the employer is willing to discriminate, there's little you can do about it, unless you have maximum evidence. If a question is illegal, you reserve the right not to answer.

## Let's Talk Money Now

185. "What sort of salary are you expecting?"

186. "The salary you're asking is near the top of the range for this job. Why should we pay you so much?"

187. "What do you think this job should pay?"

188. "When can you start?"

189. Is there anything that would stop you from taking this job if offered?"

190. "Tell me about your minimum salary expectations."

First, I want to congratulate you *in advance* for arriving at this point of the interview. I also want to congratulate you for sticking around and reading up to this point.

As you can imagine, we've finally reached the object of our labor – Da Money!

You see, there's no need working so hard to get to this point only to finally break down and go for less than you merit.

When it comes to money, employers will gladly pay you the little you ask for. All they care about is your labor. So you have to get smart at negotiating salary, especially for a high-paying job.

Remember, one of the key reasons you got to this stage of the process is because you are the best fit for the job. (By the way... NEVER talk about money while you are still in the stages of the interview process. If you are asked early in the interview what your salary expectations are, simply say: *"I think we can always come to a good compromise, if I am the chosen candidate for the job. If you think I am the best candidate, then I am ready to talk about that. Do you?"*)

So what do you say, if you know you've reached the final stage of the interview, and you're asked "What sort of salary are you expecting?"

Here are some guidelines. (Note: We are assuming here that this is a high-paying job opportunity with very little competition, where you're given the chance to negotiate):

1.  Go for a percentage of the value you can offer. Let's say you are interviewing for a sales position, and you know (and have proven in the interview) that you can bring in a *minimum* of $1,000,000 dollars in sales, annually. You can simply ask for a 10% net annual salary, which is $100,000 dollars. That boils down to about $8,333 per month. Therefore, you can start your

negotiations by opting for $9,000 or $10,000 per month. You can follow the same approach with the amount of money you can save for the employer annually.

2. What if you cannot directly quantify the value you bring in terms of cash? There is a simple way to go about that. If you have any doubts on how to personally evaluate the position, then simply ask them something like... *"Taking into consideration all the value I bring to this position, what are you ready to pay me as a salary?"* Then, take whatever amount they give you and multiply by 1.5, 2 or 3 times, and start negotiating from there.

For example, if they say *"We'll pay $4,000 per month"*, then simply say:

*"What I understand to be fair market value for this type of position, taking into consideration my unique skills and the value I bring to your business, a salary around $8,000 per month would be more appropriate. How flexible is your offer?"*

Get the idea? This is because, in more than 95% of all negotiations, the employer will always propose around half of the salary they know the position is rightfully worth (assuming you are in for a high-paying job opportunity).

**Note**: Do not mix up the benefits that are linked to actually executing the job with compensation benefits.

For example, if a car is needed to do the job, it is a service benefit that is required for the job to be done well. It is not a compensation benefit. So, don't be tricked into considering it to be a benefit. And make sure you negotiate all your service benefits first before negotiating your net compensation salary and benefits.

With that last note on "da money," I am about to end this book.

But I must say it's been a wonderful pleasure writing this book. I was actually still thinking of offering additional advice. But that will only increase the number of pages you'll be called to read.

So, the best way to keep learning about these job-getting techniques, while getting my additional support, coaching, and answers to some of your questions, is to subscribe to my free videos trainings and newsletter at:

http://JobgettingFormula.com

You can also send me your questions at:

sylvester@jobgettingformula.com

Once again, thanks for reading, and I hope I have answered most of your questions about how to get a high-paying job, as well as taught you some simple secrets and techniques that will offer you an unfair advantage over your competitors… so that you can get the high-paying job you want, to live the lifestyle you've always wanted.

Now, go get the job and let me know about your success story!

Talk soon,

Sly N.

# The Job-getting Formula

## OTHER PROGRAMS

### Some of Our Best Selling Programs

## The Job-getting Formula Online Video Training

In this 5-Step, 18 online videos program – with hand-holding, step-by-step explanations, exercises and transcripts, Sylvester walks you through how to get a high-paying job in any economy.

With Sylvester's approach, you'll finally see that there is a clear distinction between "job hunting" and actually "getting a high-paying job".

"Job hunting" is what is taught by the so-called "job hunting experts" and is mostly based on hope – they say "scatter your résumés all around the place and pray, hoping someone calls you".

The Job-getting Formula is a field-tested, practical, step-by-step, find-the-problem-and-solve-it approach. It is about figuring out and giving the employer what they want and getting a success-sized salary in return. It is really about thinking like the employer and understanding how to influence them to hire you.

Below are the different modules of the Job-getting Formula Video Training Program. For more information, visit:

http://jobgettingformula.com/OnlineVideoTraining

 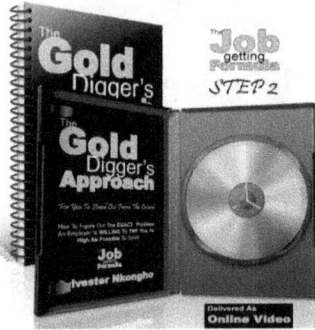

# The Goal Achiever

**There's a big difference between goal setting and goal achieving,** and Bob Proctor bridges that gap in this powerful program. Learn how to set and **achieve any goal you truly desire.** For details visit:

http://sylvesternkongho.com/portfolio.html

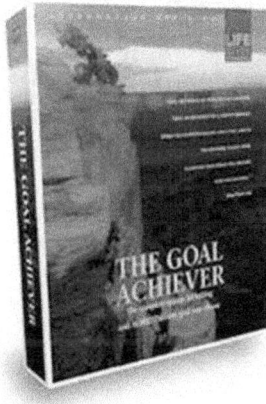

## The Winner's Image

**The Winner's Image Program** is a strong action-oriented program with powerful emphasis on accountability. Learn how to eliminate all competition from your life. Without **THIS** change, nothing else will change in your life! The Winner's Image teaches you that you can shift and choose more beneficial power in your life by shifting how you perceive yourself first. Science and psychology have isolated the one prime cause of the results you get in your life: - **the hidden image you hold of yourself.** This hidden image controls what you believe is possible for you to earn, to achieve and to deserve. For details visit:

http://sylvesternkongho.com/portfolio.html

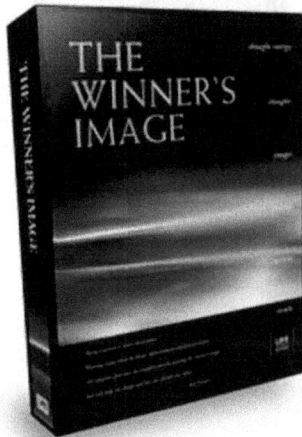

# Your Mission in Commission

As you get involved in this program, you will find yourself finally and forever stepping across the line that separates so many struggling salespeople from those who win big - month after month and year after year. You will learn the six basic concepts you MUST understand before you will ever earn large commissions.

For details visit: http://sylvesternkongho.com/portfolio.html

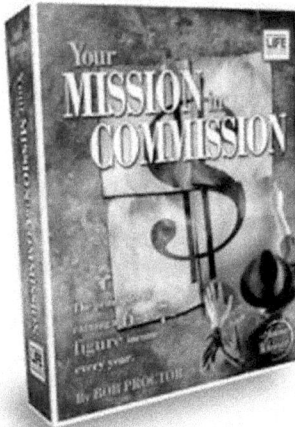

# The Success Puzzle

Sometimes, putting your life together is like trying to put a puzzle together without the cover picture on the puzzle box. How are you supposed to know how to build without a guide to help you?

In The Success Puzzle, Bob Proctor provides that step-by-step guide so that you can create the masterpiece of your life.

For details visit: http://sylvesternkongho.com/portfolio.html

# You Were Born Rich Learning System

Unlock the hidden and rich potential that allows you to achieve every financial, emotional, physical, and spiritual dream you've imagined for yourself. The Born Rich Learning System is the result of **over 27 years of intensive research** into why we behave the way we do and why we don't do many of the things we want to do.

For years Bob Proctor has studied the workings of the human mind and researched all the information he could find on the laws governing success and human potential. This program is the **most complete** exposition of his findings in the Proctor library.

For details visit: http://sylvesternkongho.com/portfolio.html

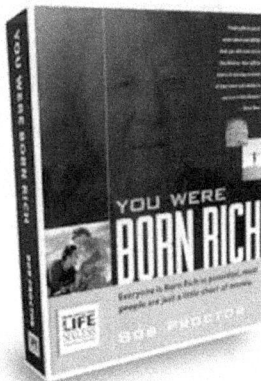

# The Job getting Formula

## *ACKNOWLEDGMENTS*

I give thanks to God for giving me the inspiration, good health, humility and strength of character to accomplish this marvelous piece of work.

Special thanks go to Stella Yufenyuy, Ellison Yufenyuy, Isidore Ashu, Violet Ako-Arrey, Donatus Ako-Arrey, Walter Takang, Emelda Wirngo, Daniel Ticha, Mbi Didier, Mbi Elvis, Magdalene Asek, Becky Enow, Magdalene Enow, Stephen Mbu, Maurice Obasi, Eyong Elvis, Serge Tampolla, Denis Ngangoum, Ange, Kingsley Nwesse, for all their great support in making this giant project a reality.

To my uncles, Ayamba Joseph and Ayamba Michael for coming to my support, whenever the going was tough. To my cousin George Oneke for standing strong by my side when things were tough.

Special thanks to my Author/Expert friends: Sama Ndango, Veronica Anderson, Nick Nanton, Lyndsay Dicks, Arielle Ford, JW Dicks, Sandra Baptiste and Stephanie Heuer for their advice and moral support.

To my sweetheart, Kelen. You went through all the toughest moments with me. Thank you for keeping the faith and love.

Thank you to my friends of AMIPO and ASSADY groups for their kind friendship and support to me personally.

And to all of you who, in one way or the other, have contributed to my success. I thank you with all my heart.

For my step-dad, Benedict Eku, I want to thank you for bringing me up in the way that made me stronger and focused on achieving success – thank you for your blessings and prayers. For my dad, Ashu Zacheus, I want to thank you for lifelong inspiration, blessings and prayers.

To my former boss, Jeanne Njenje, I thank you for kicking me out of my comfort zone forever. That was the start of my journey of "Freedom-or-Nothing-Else".

To my teachers: Napoleon Hill, Bob Proctor, Dr. Wayne Dyer, Deepak Chopra, T.B. Joshua, John Assaraf, Jack Canfield, Brian Tracy, Mark Victor Hansen, Les Brown, Jim Rohn, Zig Zigglar, Tony Robbins, Robert Kiyosaki, Eben Pagan, Frank Kern, John Carlton, Jeff Walker, Mike Filsaime. Thanks to you all.

And finally, to my mum, Elizabeth Ayuk, may your soul rest in peace, and I thank you for the seed you planted in my heart to go the extra mile and fetch what I want from life. You've been a role model to me and you continue to be for eternity.

# The Job getting Formula

## ABOUT THE AUTHOR

**Sylvester Nkongho** is an Expert, Speaker, Author, Life Success Consultant and Business Partner of Bob Proctor (star of the blockbuster movie *The Secret*). He is a proud member of America's PremierExperts®, a group of America's leading experts in various fields of Career and Business, including world renowned experts like Brian Tracy, Michael Gerber, Arielle Ford and many others. He is a holder of a master's degree in Industrial Engineering and a lover and student of spirituality, metaphysics and the mind.

He started his career working for Guinness-Diageo, a Fortune-500 multinational company. His amazing corporate profile took him from *Manufacturing & Engineering Services* to *Human Resources* to *Logistics & Distribution* to *Sales* and then *Purchasing,* where he earned the Senior Professional in Supply Management (SPSM) Certification coupled with outstanding work performance.

Working in different corporate departments, Sylvester did not only overcome the challenge of learning the trade at each stage, but greatly mastered each of them.

With such a challenging and inspiring career path for a young engineer, he had an innate calling to find answers to questions like…

**Why do many people work very hard and stay broke… while a few work effortlessly and earn millions?**

**Why do some people have it all… and others never seem to get past the starting blocks?**

**Is there a real possibility that everything you and I have been taught about Great Performance and Prosperity is so far from the truth?**

In his quest for answers, Sylvester left his salaried position with Guinness-Diageo and got coached by a man who has been studying the mind, human potential and achievement for the past 50 years…his name is Bob Proctor, you might have seen him in the movie *The Secret*.

He then became a business partner of Bob and created his own Winning Habits Coaching, Job-getting Formula Coaching, and consulting businesses, to help people achieve their personal and professional goals.

Sylvester has given keynote speeches, seminars, and one-on-one and group coaching to thousands of salespeople and other corporate employees, institutions of learning and associations based on his licensed training programs with Bob Proctor's LifeSuccess Consulting, as well as his own powerful programs on getting a high-paying job in particular, and achieving wealth, health and happiness in general.

Inspired by his life's challenges and experiences, coupled with his knowledge and experience of the POWER of Habits and the Mind in driving success, Sylvester is the Author of the "12 Habit Pillars" book entitled: **Think Rich or Die Poor:** *Why Are Winners Always Attracting Riches… And The 12 Secret Habits You Must Develop If You Ever Want To Become A Winner!*

Sylvester's Interview on **Meet the Experts with Arielle Ford** about his book has been featured on **ABC**, **CBS**, **NBC** and **FOX** affiliates in the United States.

Meet Sylvester and receive free job-getting video training at www.JobgettingFormula.com.

Meet Sylvester and receive free job-getting video training at
www.JobgettingFormula.com